Daily Paragraph Editing

GRADE 7

Writing: Emily Hutchinson
Content Editing: Robin Kelly
Lisa Vitarisi Mathews
Teera Safi
Copy Editing: Cathy Harber
Art Direction: Cheryl Puckett
Art Resources: Kathy Kopp
Cover Design: Cheryl Puckett
Design/Production: Carolina Caird
Susan Lovell

EMC 2837

Evan-Moor®
Helping Children Learn

Visit
teaching-standards.com
to view a correlation
of this book.
This is a free service.

Correlated to State and Common Core State Standards

Congratulations on your purchase of some of the finest teaching materials in the world.

For information about other Evan-Moor products, call 1-800-777-4362, fax 1-800-777-4332, or visit our Web site, www.evan-moor.com.
Entire contents © 2013 EVAN-MOOR CORP.
18 Lower Ragsdale Drive, Monterey, CA 93940-5746. Printed in USA.

CPSIA: Printed by McNaughton & Gunn, Saline, MI USA.[2/2015]

Contents

Friday Writing Prompts

Introduction

Why Daily Paragraph Editing?

This book is designed to help students master and retain grade-level skills in language mechanics and expression through focused, daily practice. The passages represent the writing forms that students encounter in their daily reading and writing activities across the curriculum. A weekly writing activity allows students to apply the skills they have been practicing throughout the week.

What's in This Book?

Daily Paragraph Editing contains lessons for 36 weeks, with a separate lesson for each day. Each week's lessons for Monday through Thursday consist of individual reproducible paragraphs that contain errors in the following skills:

- capitalization
- language usage
- punctuation
- spelling, and more

Each Friday lesson consists of a writing prompt that directs students to write in response to the week's composition. This gives students the opportunity to apply the skills they have practiced during the week in their own writing. Students gain experience writing in a variety of forms, with the support of familiar models.

How Does It Work?

Students correct the errors in each daily portion of the composition by marking directly on the page. A reproducible sheet of Proofreading Marks (see page 168) helps familiarize students with the standard form for marking corrections on written text. Full-page Editing Keys show corrections for all errors. Error Summaries help teachers identify the targeted skills in each week's lessons so teachers can plan to review or introduce the specific skills needed by their students.

A reproducible Language Handbook (pages 169–176) outlines the usage and mechanics rules for students to follow as they edit. The Handbook includes examples to help familiarize students with how the conventions of language and mechanics are applied in authentic writing.

When corrected and read together, the paragraphs that make up the week's lesson form a cohesive composition that also serves as a writing model for students. The compositions cover a broad range of expository and narrative writing forms from across the curriculum, including the following:

- nonfiction texts on grade-level topics in science and social studies
- biographies, book reviews, persuasive essays, journal entries, and letters
- myths, fables, historical fiction, personal narratives, and realistic fiction

Student's daily lesson pages for Monday through Thursday

Indicates the writing form modeled in the weekly lesson

Identifies the day and week

Provides text with errors for students to correct

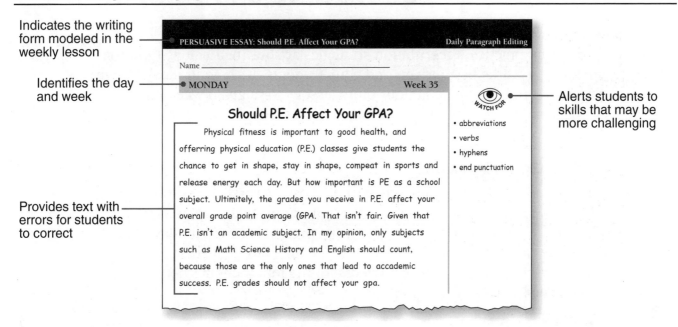

Alerts students to skills that may be more challenging

Friday writing prompts

Identifies the week

Prompts students to write a composition in the same form as the weekly lesson

Provides sample lead sentences to support reluctant writers

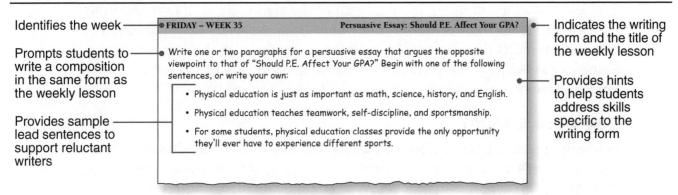

Indicates the writing form and the title of the weekly lesson

Provides hints to help students address skills specific to the writing form

Teacher's full-sized annotated Editing Key

Indicates the writing form modeled in the weekly lesson

Identifies the day and week

Shows the student text with corrections marked in red. (See page 168 for proofreading marks.)

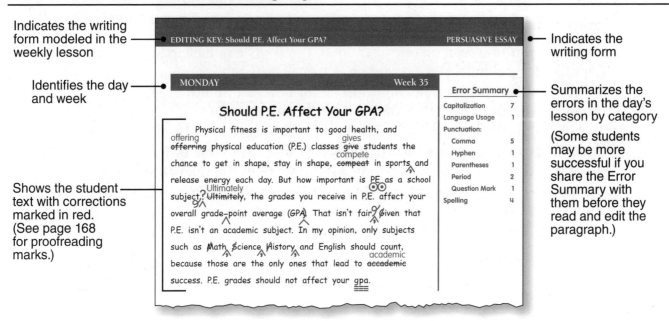

Indicates the writing form

Summarizes the errors in the day's lesson by category

(Some students may be more successful if you share the Error Summary with them before they read and edit the paragraph.)

How to Use *Daily Paragraph Editing*

You can use *Daily Paragraph Editing* with the whole class or assign lessons for individual practice. Presentation strategies are outlined below. Find the approach that works best for you and your students. It's a good idea, though, to reproduce and distribute all four daily lessons for a given week on Monday. That way, students can use the previous day's lesson for reference as the week progresses.

Directed Group Lessons

The *Daily Paragraph Editing* lessons will be most successful if you introduce each one as a group activity. Have students mark up their copies as you work through the lesson together. Continue presenting the Monday through Thursday lessons to the entire class until you are confident that students are familiar with the editing process. Try one of the following methods to direct group lessons:

Option 1

Display the day's editing lesson using a projection system. Read the text aloud just as it is written, including all of the errors. Read it a second time, using phrasing and intonation that would be appropriate if all punctuation were correct. Guide students in correcting errors; mark the corrections on the displayed page. Encourage students to discuss the reason for each correction; explain or clarify any rules that are unfamiliar.

Option 2

Display the day's lesson using a projection system. Work with students to focus on one type of error at a time, correcting all errors of the same type (e.g., capitalization, commas, subject/verb agreement, spelling). Refer to the Error Summary in the Editing Key to help you identify the various types of errors.

Option 3

Conduct a mini-lesson on one or more of the skills emphasized in that day's lesson—for example, run-on sentences or commas to separate coordinate adjectives. This is especially appropriate for new or unfamiliar skills, or for skills that are especially challenging or confusing for students (such as misplaced or dangling modifiers). After introducing a specific skill, use the approach outlined in Option 2 to focus on that skill in one or more of the week's daily paragraphs. To provide additional practice, refer to the Skills Scope & Sequence (pages 9 and 10) to find other compositions that include that target skill.

Individual Practice

Once students are familiar with the process for editing the daily paragraphs, they may work on their own or with a partner to make corrections. Be sure students have their Proofreading Marks available to help them mark their corrections. Remind students to refer to the student Language Handbook as needed for guidance in the rules of mechanics and usage. Some students may find it helpful to know at the outset the number and types of errors they are seeking. Provide this information by referring to the Error Summary on the annotated Editing Key pages.

Customizing Instruction

Some of the skills covered in *Daily Paragraph Editing* may not be part of the grade-level expectancies in the language program you use. Some skills may even be taught differently in your program from the way they are modeled in *Daily Paragraph Editing*. In such cases, follow the approach used in your program. Simply revise the paragraph text as needed (using correction fluid or tape and then writing changes) before you reproduce pages for students.

Occasionally, you or your students may make a correction that differs from that shown in the Editing Key. The decision to use an exclamation mark instead of a period, or a period instead of a semicolon, is often a subjective decision made by individual writers. When discrepancies of this sort arise, capitalize on the "teachable moment" to let students know that there are gray areas in English usage and mechanics, and discuss how each of the possible correct choices can affect the meaning or tone of the writing.

Using the Writing Prompts

Have students keep their daily lessons in a folder so they can review the week's corrected paragraphs on Friday. Identify the writing form modeled in the composition and any of its special features (e.g., dialogue in fiction, an opinion statement in a persuasive essay, or a salutation in a letter).

Present the Friday writing prompt using a projection system, or distribute copies to students. Take a few minutes to brainstorm ideas with the group and to focus on language skills that students will need to address in their writing.

After students have completed their writing, encourage them to use an editing checklist (see page 8 for ideas) to review or revise their work. You may also want to have partners review each other's writing. To conduct a more formal assessment of students' writing, use the Assessment Rubric on page 11.

If you assign paragraph writing as homework, make sure that students have the daily lessons (with corrections) for that week available for reference. Students may need to reflect on the content as well as the form to complete the writing assignment.

Creating an Editing Checklist

You may want to develop an editing checklist with the class. Post the checklist in the classroom and encourage students to use it as they revise their own writing or critique a partner's efforts. Here are some items for your checklist:

- Does each proper noun begin with a capital letter?
- Does each sentence end with a period, a question mark, or an exclamation point?
- Did I use an apostrophe correctly in a contraction?
- Did I use an apostrophe correctly to show possession?
- Did I place commas where they are needed?
- Did I use the correct word of two or more homonyms?
- Does the verb in each sentence agree with the subject?
- Are my sentences clear and complete?
- Are there any spelling errors?

Assessment Rubric for Evaluating Friday Paragraph Writing

The Friday writing prompts give students the opportunity to apply the capitalization, punctuation, and language usage skills they practiced during the week's editing tasks. They also require students to write in a variety of forms.

In evaluating the Friday paragraphs, you may want to focus exclusively on students' mastery of mechanics and usage, or you may want to conduct a more global assessment of their writing. The rubric on page 11 offers broad guidelines for evaluating the composition as a whole. You may want to share the rubric with students so they know what is expected of them.

Skills Scope and Sequence

Weeks

Capitalization	1	2	3	4	5	6	7	8	9	10	11	12	13	14	15	16	17	18	19	20	21	22	23	24	25	26	27	28	29	30	31	32	33	34	35	36
Beginning of sentences, quotations, salutations/closings	●	●	●	●	●	●	●	●	●	●	●	●	●	●	●	●	●	●	●	●	●	●	●	●	●	●	●	●	●	●	●	●	●	●	●	●
Days and months				●		●	●			●			●	●		●	●			●				●					●	●			●			
Holidays, historic events, eras, historical documents																●		●					●						●							●
Inappropriate capitalization	●			●			●	●		●		●					●	●	●	●	●	●	●	●	●	●	●	●	●		●	●		●	●	●
Initials, acronyms, abbreviations	●			●			●			●	●												●					●								
Names and titles, languages, nationalities, geographic identities	●	●	●	●	●	●	●	●	●			●			●	●	●						●					●	●		●	●	●	●	●	●
Nouns used as names (Aunt, Grandpa, etc.)						●			●																											
Place names, organizations, other proper nouns	●	●	●	●		●	●	●				●			●						●	●							●	●	●	●		●		●
Titles of books, magazines, stories, movies, TV shows																			●																	●

Language Usage	1	2	3	4	5	6	7	8	9	10	11	12	13	14	15	16	17	18	19	20	21	22	23	24	25	26	27	28	29	30	31	32	33	34	35	36
Adverbs	●	●		●									●		●								●				●			●				●	●	
Articles	●				●	●	●			●					●	●	●	●			●	●		●		●	●		●	●	●		●	●	●	●
Commonly mistaken words (affect/effect, then/than, etc.)			●		●	●	●		●	●			●	●				●	●		●					●	●	●	●			●	●	●	●	●
Comparative and superlative adjectives				●			●	●						●		●												●				●				
Inappropriate double negatives	●								●					●																						
Pronouns and possessives (its, our, whose, etc.)	●		●	●	●		●	●	●			●										●	●				●			●	●			●	●	●
Subject-verb agreement and plural usage	●		●	●	●			●		●		●			●	●	●				●	●			●	●	●	●	●	●	●	●	●	●	●	●
Verbs and verb tenses, including irregular and passive forms	●			●	●	●	●	●	●	●	●	●	●			●	●	●	●	●	●	●		●	●	●	●	●	●			●	●	●	●	●

Punctuation: Apostrophes	1	2	3	4	5	6	7	8	9	10	11	12	13	14	15	16	17	18	19	20	21	22	23	24	25	26	27	28	29	30	31	32	33	34	35	36
To form contractions			●	●	●	●	●	●	●	●	●	●	●	●	●	●	●	●	●	●	●	●	●	●	●	●	●	●	●	●	●	●	●	●	●	●
To form possessives	●		●	●	●	●	●		●	●	●	●	●	●	●	●	●	●	●	●	●	●	●	●	●	●	●	●	●	●	●	●	●	●	●	●
Improperly placed apostrophes	●		●	●				●											●																	

Punctuation: Commas	1	2	3	4	5	6	7	8	9	10	11	12	13	14	15	16	17	18	19	20	21	22	23	24	25	26	27	28	29	30	31	32	33	34	35	36
After introductory interjections or expressions			●	●	●			●	●					●					●		●									●	●					●
After introductory words or phrases	●		●	●	●				●				●			●	●			●			●	●	●	●	●	●	●	●		●	●	●	●	●
After salutation and closing in a letter																					●		●													
Between city and state, city and country names									●			●			●		●											●								●
Between items in a series	●	●	●	●	●		●	●	●	●	●	●	●			●		●	●	●	●	●	●	●	●	●	●	●	●	●		●	●	●		●
Improperly placed comma	●	●			●			●			●		●																		●					
In complex sentences			●	●	●			●		●	●	●	●		●	●				●		●	●	●	●	●	●	●	●	●	●	●	●	●	●	●
In compound sentences	●		●	●	●	●	●	●	●	●	●	●	●	●	●	●	●	●	●	●	●	●	●	●	●	●	●	●	●	●	●	●	●	●	●	●
In dates					●												●							●												
To separate coordinate adjectives		●	●						●																			●	●							●
To set off appositives	●		●					●	●	●			●		●	●	●					●			●		●			●		●				●

Skills Scope and Sequence (continued)

Weeks

Skill	1	2	3	4	5	6	7	8	9	10	11	12	13	14	15	16	17	18	19	20	21	22	23	24	25	26	27	28	29	30	31	32	33	34	35	36
Punctuation: Commas (continued)																																				
To set off interruptions	●		●		●	●	●			●		●	●	●	●	●	●	●	●	●	●	●	●	●		●	●		●	●		●	●	●	●	●
To set off quotations				●		●			●		●											●			●		●	●		●	●					
With name used in direct address				●					●															●												
Punctuation: Periods																																				
At end of sentence	●	●	●	●	●	●	●	●	●	●	●	●	●	●	●	●	●	●	●	●	●	●	●	●	●	●	●	●	●	●	●	●	●	●	●	●
Improperly placed period								●					●						●							●						●				
In abbreviations of names, measurements, scientific names, etc.			●			●									●			●					●					●				●		●		●
Punctuation: Quotation Marks																																				
Improperly placed quotation mark	●		●								●					●			●				●	●	●					●	●					
In dialogue, speech, excerpts						●	●		●		●											●			●			●		●	●		●			●
To set apart special words or phrases	●		●											●										●			●	●								
With titles of articles, poems, short stories, songs, etc.																		●								●						●				
Punctuation: Other																																				
Colon to show time										●					●																					
Ellipses for pause or omission														●										●				●					●			
Exclamation point				●							●			●					●		●			●							●					
Hyphen in fractions			●	●								●																								
Hyphen to form adjectives or spelled-out numbers						●			●	●		●				●			●	●	●				●					●		●	●		●	●
Improperly placed hyphen									●																●								●			
Parentheses and brackets		●				●	●						●				●					●					●		●							●
Punctuation inside quotation marks						●			●		●		●							●		●			●				●	●		●			●	●
Punctuation with parentheses or brackets				●					●										●					●						●		●				●
Question mark			●					●			●		●	●	●				●			●				●		●	●	●	●	●		●	●	●
Semicolon to join two independent clauses		●																													●				●	
Underline scientific names, foreign words, ship names, etc.	●				●										●																		●			●
Underline titles of books, magazines, movies, newspapers, etc.																								●								●				●
Sentence Structure																																				
Misplaced and dangling modifiers																		●																●		
Spelling																																				
Identify errors in grade-level words	●	●	●	●	●	●	●	●	●	●	●	●	●	●	●	●	●	●	●	●	●	●	●	●	●	●	●	●	●	●	●	●	●	●	●	●

Daily Paragraph Editing • EMC 2837 • © Evan-Moor Corp.

Assessment Rubric

	EXCELLENT	GOOD	FAIR	WEAK
Clarity and Focus	Writing is exceptionally clear, focused, and interesting.	Writing is generally clear, focused, and interesting.	Writing is loosely focused on the topic.	Writing is unclear and unfocused.
Development of Main Ideas	Main ideas are clear, specific, and well-developed.	Main ideas are identifiable but may be somewhat general.	Main ideas are overly broad or simplistic.	Main ideas are unclear or not expressed.
Organization	Organization is clear (beginning, middle, and end) and fits the topic and writing form.	Organization is clear but may be predictable or formulaic.	Organization is attempted but is often unclear.	Organization is not coherent.
Use of Details	Details are relevant, specific, and well-placed.	Details are relevant but may be overly general.	Details may be off-topic, predictable, or not specific enough.	Details are absent or insufficient to support main ideas.
Vocabulary	Vocabulary is exceptionally rich, varied, and well-chosen.	Vocabulary is colorful and generally avoids clichés.	Vocabulary is ordinary and may rely on clichés.	Vocabulary is limited, general, or vague.
Mechanics and Usage	Demonstrates exceptionally strong command of conventions of punctuation, capitalization, spelling, and usage.	Demonstrates adequate control of conventions of punctuation, capitalization, spelling, and usage.	Errors in the conventions of mechanics and language usage distract but do not impede the reader.	Limited ability to control conventions of mechanics and language usage impairs readability of the composition.

MONDAY   Week 1

Artful Defense

A martial art is a system of self-~~defents~~ defense that can also be a competitive sport. People ~~practices~~ practice martial arts for physical ~~fitnes~~ fitness, mental ~~dissiplin~~ discipline, spiritual ~~developpment~~ development, and other reasons. Some martial arts, such as tai chi (ty chee), also ~~teaches~~ teach(Think) healing skills, including deep ~~breatheing~~ breathing and meditation. Most martial arts practiced today, including judo, karate, and jujitsu, ~~has~~ have their origins in China, korea, or japan. In modern times, asian and american ~~moovies~~ movies have increased the popularity of martial arts. This essay looks at two popular forms of martial arts: taekwondo and kung fu.

Error Summary

Capitalization	4
Language Usage	3
Punctuation:	
Comma	2
Period	1
Spelling	6

TUESDAY   Week 1

Taekwondo is a Korean art of unarmed combat. The korean word taekwondo ~~mean~~ means "~~methid~~ method of kicking or punching." This modern sport has ancient roots but was ~~name~~ named only in 1955. Thirty ~~milyun~~ million people world wide practice this popular sport. Students of Taekwondo learn to ~~delliver~~ deliver fast, powerful, and high kicks, sometimes while spinning or jumping. They also ~~learns~~ learn to strike with ~~they~~ their fists and to block, or avoid, an opponents kick or hit. When partners spar, or practice together, they kick or strike without completely ~~makeing~~ making ~~contack~~ contact. That way, they don't hurt each other. ~~Indivijiuls~~ Individuals can also practice by using a ~~targete~~ target.

Error Summary

Capitalization	2
Language Usage	4
Punctuation:	
Apostrophe	1
Comma	2
Spelling	8

Name _____

| MONDAY | Week 1 |

Artful Defense

A martial art is a system of self-defents that can also be a competitive sport. People practices martial arts for physical fitnes, mental dissiplin, spiritual developpment, and other reasons. Some martial arts, such as tai chi (ty chee), also teaches healing skills, including deep breatheing and meditation. Most martial arts practiced today, including judo, karate, and jujitsu, has their origins in China korea or japan. In modern times, asian and american moovies have increased the popularity of martial arts. This essay looks at two popular forms of martial arts: taekwondo and kung fu

• place names
• cultural identities
• verbs

| TUESDAY | Week 1 |

Taekwondo is a Korean art of unarmed combat. The korean word <u>taekwondo</u> mean "methid of kicking or punching." This modern sport has ancient roots but was name only in 1955. Thirty milyun people world wide practice this popular sport. Students of Taekwondo learn to delliver fast powerful and high kicks, sometimes while spinning or jumping. They also learns to strike with they fists and to block, or avoid, an opponents kick or hit. When partners spar, or practice together, they kick or strike without completely makeing contack. That way, they don't hurt each other. Indivijiuls can also practice by using a targete.

• names of languages
• verbs
• commas
• possessives

WEDNESDAY   Week 1

Like taekwondo, kung fu is mostly an unarmed form of combat. Kung fu, also called wushu⌃was developed more than 2,000 years ago in c̲hina. The c̲hinese word <u>kung fu</u> means "skill gained from hard work." The original ~~meening~~ ^{meaning} refers to any skill, not just to martial arts. The Chinese word <u>wushu,</u>^{though} ~~thogh~~, means "martial arts."

Kung fu students ~~lern~~ ^{learn} poses and meditation as well as how to kick⌃ punch⌃ throw⌃ jump⌃ and roll. Some techniques ^{imitate} ~~immitate~~ the movements of animals such as tigers⌃ snakes⌃ and leopards. There are hundreds of kung fu styles; some ^{styles} ~~stiles~~ include ^{weapons} ~~wepons~~ such as swords and sticks.

Error Summary

Capitalization	2
Punctuation:	
Comma	7
Quotation Mark	1
Underlined Words	1
Spelling	6

THURSDAY   Week 1

Taekwondo and kung fu are both martial arts⌃ but there ^{are} ~~is~~ many differences between them. One is k̲orean, and one is Chinese. Both ~~has~~ ^{have} ~~ainshunt~~ ^{ancient} origins, but kung fu is older. Both ~~involves~~ ^{involve} kicking, punching⌃ and jumping⌃ although kung fu can include weapons. Both ~~is~~ ^{are} competitive sports, each with ~~strick~~ ^{strict} rules so ~~participints~~ ^{participants} don't get ~~injerd~~ ^{injured}. Taekwondo ~~have~~ ^{has} a formal system of ranking, with different belt colors to ~~indecate~~ ^{indicate} the level. What matters most in kung fu is how many years students study and how hard they practice⊙ Perhaps most important⌃ people can practice either of these martial arts for fitness, self-discipline, and ~~iner~~ ^{inner} strength.

Error Summary

Capitalization	1
Language Usage	5
Punctuation:	
Comma	4
Period	1
Spelling	6

Name _____

WEDNESDAY   Week 1

- place names
- words that are defined
- foreign words

Like taekwondo, kung fu is mostly an unarmed form of combat. Kung fu, also called wushu was developed more than 2,000 years ago in china. The chinese word <u>kung fu</u> means "skill gained from hard work." The original meening refers to any skill, not just to martial arts. The Chinese word wushu, thogh, means martial arts."

Kung fu students lern poses and meditation as well as how to kick punch throw jump and roll. Some techniques immitate the movements of animals such as tigers snakes and leopards. There are hundreds of kung fu styles; some stiles include wepons such as swords and sticks.

THURSDAY   Week 1

- commas
- verbs
- end punctuation

Taekwondo and kung fu are both martial arts but there is many differences between them. One is korean, and one is Chinese. Both has ainshunt origins, but kung fu is older. Both involves kicking, punching and jumping although kung fu can include weapons. Both is competitive sports, each with strick rules so participints don't get injerd. Taekwondo have a formal system of ranking, with different belt colors to indecate the level. What matters most in kung fu is how many years students study and how hard they practice? Perhaps most important people can practice either of these martial arts for fitness, self-discipline, and iner strength.

MONDAY	Week 2

Error Summary

Capitalization	5
Language Usage	2
Punctuation:	
Apostrophe	1
Comma	4
Period	1
Spelling	4

How to Use Chopsticks

Chopsticks originated in China about 5,000 years ago. They are still the most common eating utensils through out china, japan, korea, and Vietnam, as well as in many regions where chinese immigrants settled. People who are ~~acustemmed~~ accustomed to using forks, knives, and spoons sometimes find it difficult at first to use chopsticks. With practice, though, anyone can master their use. Chopsticks are a pinching type of ~~utensul~~ utensil so it's a good idea to practice with bite-sized foods or sticky foods, like sushi, that ~~is~~ are easy to pick up. ~~Largest~~ Larger foods, such as steak, are ~~awkwerd~~ awkward to pick up with pinchers.

TUESDAY	Week 2

Error Summary

Capitalization	3
Language Usage	2
Punctuation:	
Comma	1
Period	1
Quotation Mark	2
Spelling	7

To master the use of chopsticks, ~~folew~~ follow these steps:

1. Hold the first chopstick near the middle of the stick, with the narrow part pointing down like the tip of a pencil.

2. ~~Ajust~~ Adjust your finger ~~positiun~~ position so the narrow part of the stick is against the tips of your middle and ring fingers. The wider end will rest near the ~~knuckel~~ knuckle of your index finger. Press against the stick with your ~~thum~~ thumb.

3. Pick up the "second" chopstick and ~~held~~ hold it between the tip of your index finger and the ~~tib~~ tip of your thumb.

4. bend or extend ~~you're~~ your index finger to move the second chopstick. the first chopstick should ~~not~~ never move.

Name _____

| MONDAY | Week 2 |

- commas
- place names

How to Use Chopsticks

Chopsticks originated in China about 5,000 years ago. They are still the most common eating utensils through out china, japan, korea, and Vietnam, as well as in many regions where chinese immigrants settled. People who are acustemmed to using forks knives and spoons sometimes find it difficult at first to use chopsticks. With practice, though anyone can master their use. Chopsticks are a pinching type of utensul so its a good idea to practice with bite-sized foods or sticky foods, like sushi, that is easy to pick up. Largest foods, such as Steak, are awkwerd to pick up with pinchers

| TUESDAY | Week 2 |

- commas
- quotation marks
- double negatives

To master the use of chopsticks, folow these steps:
1. Hold the first chopstick near the middle of the stick, with the narrow part pointing down like the tip of a pencil.
2. Ajust your finger positiun so the narrow part of the stick is against the tips of your middle, and ring fingers. The wider end will rest near the knuckel of your Index finger. Press against the stick with your thum.
3. Pick up the "second" chopstick and held it between the tip of your index finger and the tib of your thumb
4. bend or extend you're index finger to move the second chopstick. the first chopstick should not never move.

WEDNESDAY   Week 2

Here are some ~~aditional~~ additional tips to keep in mind as you practice. They will help you use chopsticks with ~~confidense~~ confidence.

1. Line up the ends of your chopsticks so they are even. That way, the tips will come together when they ~~closes~~ close, allowing you to grab ~~bitts~~ bits of food more ~~easy~~ easily. It also ~~prevent~~ prevents the chopsticks from crossing each other and forming ~~a~~ an X.

2. Tilt your wrist at an ~~angel~~ angle, as if you ~~was~~ were using a spoon. Dont hold your chopsticks ~~verticly~~ vertically.

3. Don't use your pinky finger (the ~~littler~~ littlest finger) as you grip the chopsticks. Instead, relax that finger.

Error Summary

Capitalization	1
Language Usage	6
Punctuation:	
Apostrophe	1
Period	1
Spelling	5

THURSDAY   Week 2

Its also important to adhere to certain rules of etiquette when using ~~chopstix~~ chopsticks. The following actions ~~is~~ are considered rude and could ~~affend~~ offend fellow diners. Avoid:

• stabbing or spearing food with your chopsticks

• ~~scouping~~ scooping up food (except Rice) with your chopsticks

• pulling or ~~pushin~~ pushing a dish with your chopstick's

• sucking on or biting your chopsticks

• pointing with your chopsticks, gesturing with them or ~~waveing~~ waving them around

• placing chopsticks ~~upwrite~~ upright in ~~an~~ a bowl of rice

• laying your chopsticks directly on the ~~tabble~~ table

Error Summary

Capitalization	1
Language Usage	2
Punctuation:	
Apostrophe	2
Comma	1
Parentheses	1
Spelling	7

Name _____

WEDNESDAY   Week 2

Here are some aditional tips to keep in mind as you practice. They will help you use chopsticks with confidense.

1. Line up the ends of your chopsticks so they are even. That way, the tips will come together when they closes, allowing you to grab bitts of food more easy It also prevent the chopsticks from crossing each other and forming a X.

2. Tilt your wrist at an angel, as if you was using a spoon. Dont hold your chopsticks verticly.

3. Don't use your pinky finger (the littler finger) as you grip the Chopsticks. Instead, relax that finger.

- apostrophes
- adverbs
- articles
- verbs

THURSDAY   Week 2

Its also important to adhere to certain rules of etiquette when using chopstix. The following actions is considered rude and could affend fellow diners. Avoid:

- stabbing or spearing food with your chopsticks
- scouping up food (except Rice with your chopsticks
- pulling or pushin a dish with your chopstick's
- sucking on or biting your chopsticks
- pointing with your chopsticks, gesturing with them or waveing them around
- placing chopsticks upwrite in an bowl of rice
- laying your chopsticks directly on the tabble

- parentheses
- apostrophes
- verbs

leave yourr [context]
- emigrate fn
immigrate — to enter + settle.

MONDAY   Week 3

Immigration and Ellis Island

occurred
The greatest mass movement of people in ~~H~~istory ~~occurred~~ between 1870 and 1910. During that time, more

emigrated
than twenty million people ~~emmigrated~~ from europe to the

united states. People left their homelands for many reasons Historians call these reasons "pushes". Pushes include natural

disasters
~~dissasters~~ crop failures war persecution and poverty. A push

might also be the urge for adventure or the desire for

change. People who emigrate go to places where they think

they will have a better happier future for themselves and

their
~~they're~~ families. Historians call these reasons "pulls".

Error Summary

Capitalization	4
Punctuation:	
Comma	5
Period	1
Quotation Mark	3
Spelling	4

TUESDAY   Week 3

Between 1870 and 1900 about twelve million people

arrived in the United States from other countries. Most

came from europe. Another nine million arrived over the next

previous
decade (three-fourths as many as during the ~~prevous~~ three

decades). Most immigrants entered the country through new

allowed
York. Before they were ~~aloud~~ into the city they had to go

through
~~threw~~ the immigration center located on ellis island which is

in Upper New York Bay. The statue of liberty in the bay

seemed to welcome the passengers. Not everyone however

was   inspectors
~~were~~ truly welcome. The ~~inspecters~~ at Ellis Island would

who
decide ~~whom~~ could enter the country

Error Summary

Capitalization	6
Language Usage	2
Punctuation:	
Comma	5
Hyphen	1
Period	1
Spelling	4

Name _____   Isnt Sayula

| MONDAY | Week 3 |

Immigration and Ellis Island

The greatest mass movement of people in History ocurred between 1870 and 1910. During that time, more than twenty million people emmigrated from europe to the united states. People left their homelands for many reasons Historians call these reasons "pushes". Pushes include natural dissasters crop failures war persecution and poverty. A push might also be the urge for adventure or the desire for change. People who emigrate go to places where they think they will have a better happier future for themselves and they're families. Historians call these reasons pulls.

WATCH FOR
- commas
- place names
- punctuation with quotation marks
- special words in quotation marks

| TUESDAY | Week 3 |

Between 1870 and 1900 about twelve million people arrived in the United States from other countries. Most came from europe. Another nine million arrived over the next decade (three fourths as many as during the prevous three decades). Most immigrants entered the country through new York. Before they were aloud into the city they had to go threw the immigration center located on ellis island which is in Upper New York Bay. The statue of liberty in the bay seemed to welcome the passengers. Not everyone however were truly welcome. The inspecters at Ellis Island would decide whom could enter the country

WATCH FOR
- names of monuments
- hyphens
- pronouns

WEDNESDAY   Week 3

Ellis Island was named for its original owner, a man
by the name of samuel ellis. he operated a ~~tavvern~~ *tavern* for local
~~fisherman~~ *fishermen* on the island. Before that, the sandy ~~peace~~ *piece* of land
was known to new yorkers as gibbet island. a gibbet was a
gallows-like structure from which criminals, such as pirates,
were hanged. Occasionally in the 1700s, pirates were hanged
from trees on the islands ~~shor~~ *shore*. Earlier, the island was known
by other names. The dutch ~~collonists~~ *colonists* who settled in new
york around 1630 called the island oyster island because of
the nearby ~~oister~~ *oyster* beds, which had been a ~~souce~~ *source* of food for
people in the area for many decades.

Error Summary

Capitalization	13
Language Usage	1
Punctuation:	
Apostrophe	1
Comma	4
Period	2
Spelling	6

THURSDAY   Week 3

the federal ~~goverment~~ *government* took over the island in 1892.
From that time until 1954, when the immigration center
~~clozed~~ *closed*, twelve million immigrants ~~past~~ *passed* through ellis island:
four-fifths of all immigrants entering the country. Thats
astonishing! So, what was the immigrant ~~expereince~~ *experience* like? First,
immigrants entered a huge hall and left ~~they're~~ *their* bags. Then
they lined up and filed ~~passed~~ *past* inspectors. If rejected, they
could be sent back to their home countries. Most, however,
passed through the center within hours. Ferries ran back and
~~fourth~~ *forth* around the clock, taking the immigrants to manhattan
to start their new lives in america.

Error Summary

Capitalization	5
Punctuation:	
Apostrophe	1
Comma	2
Exclamation Point	1
Hyphen	1
Question Mark	1
Spelling	7

Name _____ *I sent Sapula*

WEDNESDAY   Week 3

Ellis Island was named for its original owner a man by the name of samuel ellis he operated a tavvern for local fisherman on the island. Before that, the sandy peace of land was known to new yorkers as gibbet island a gibbet was a gallows-like structure from which criminals, such as pirates were hanged. Occasionally in the 1700s, pirates were hanged from trees on the islands shor. Earlier the island was known by other names. The dutch collonists who settled in new york around 1630 called the island oyster island because of the nearby oister beds which had been a souce of food for people in the area for many decades.

WATCH FOR

• place names
• personal names
• geographic identities
• run-on sentences

THURSDAY   Week 3

the federal goverment took over the island in 1892. From that time until 1954, when the immigration center clozed, twelve million immigrants past through ellis island: four fifths of all immigrants entering the country. Thats astonishing So, what was the immigrant expereince like. First, immigrants entered a huge hall and left they're bags. Then they lined up and filed passed inspectors. If rejected, they could be sent back to their home countries. Most however passed through the center within hours. Ferries ran back and fourth around the clock, taking the immigrants to manhattan to start their new lives in america.

WATCH FOR

• place names
• commas
• hyphens
• end punctuation

MONDAY   Week 4

Echo and Narcissus

Mount Olympus was home to the greek gods. Zeus
was ~~cheif~~ chief of the gods. The ~~sacrid~~ sacred Mount Helicon was home
to the nymphs, whose job was to tend to Zeus's wife Hera.
When the nymphs were not working, they liked to play near
the ~~sparkeling~~ sparkling waterfalls and wooded ~~forrests~~ forests at the base of
Mount Helicon. Of all the nymphs, Echo was the ~~merrier~~ merriest and
also the ~~better~~ best storyteller. Sometimes Echo would ~~ammuse~~ amuse
Hera while Zeus came down from Mount Olympus to join the
nymphs in their ~~advenchures~~ adventures. Echo's stories kept the ~~godess~~ goddess
occupied so she would forget to be ~~jealus~~ jealous.

Error Summary

Capitalization	1
Language Usage	2
Punctuation:	
Apostrophe	1
Comma	2
Spelling	8

TUESDAY   Week 4

Among the nymphs, Echo was one of Hera's favorite's.
Perhaps that's why the goddess was so ~~easy~~ easily tricked by her.
Hera would smile ~~calm~~ calmly at Echo and ask "What tale do you
have for me today? Echo, sitting at Hera's feet, would begin
to spin her tale. Her stories and her chatter ~~was~~ were always
entertaining, and the time would slip by ~~quick~~ quickly as Hera
~~lissened~~ listened. Meanwhile, Echo's ~~freinds~~ friends enjoyed themselves without
worrying that Hera would interrupt them. One day, Hera
discovered Echo's trick. Full of wrath, she cried, "how dare
you ~~decieve~~ deceive me in this way! I have a ~~speshul~~ special punishment for
you! Do you want to ~~here~~ hear what it is?"

Error Summary

Capitalization	1
Language Usage	4
Punctuation:	
Apostrophe	4
Comma	2
Exclamation Point	1
Question Mark	2
Quotation Mark	4
Spelling	5

Name _____

Echo and Narcissus

Mount Olympus was home to the greek gods. Zeus was cheif of the gods. The sacrid Mount Helicon was home to the nymphs, whose job was to tend to Zeus's wife Hera. When the nymphs were not working, they liked to play near the sparkeling waterfalls and wooded forrests at the base of Mount Helicon. Of all the nymphs Echo was the merrier and also the better storyteller. Sometimes Echo would ammuse Hera while Zeus came down from Mount Olympus to join the nymphs in their advenchures. Echos stories kept the godess occupied so she would forget to be jealus.

- nationalities
- apostrophes
- words that compare

Among the nymphs, Echo was one of Heras favorite's. Perhaps thats why the goddess was so easy tricked by her. Hera would smile calm at Echo and ask What tale do you have for me today. Echo, sitting at Hera's feet would begin to spin her tale. Her stories and her chatter was always entertaining, and the time would slip by quick as Hera lissened. Meanwhile, Echo's freinds enjoyed themselves without worrying that Hera would interrupt them. One day, Hera discovered Echos trick. Full of wrath, she cried, how dare you decieve me in this way I have a speshul punishment for you! Do you want to here what it is.

- apostrophes
- dialogue
- end punctuation
- adverbs

WEDNESDAY　　　　　　　　　　　　　　　Week 4

The ~~frightend~~ *frightened* Echo simply nodded. Hera continued to proclaim ~~angry~~ *angrily*, "The gift that you have used to trick me shall be yours no longer! From this moment on you will not be able to speak until someone else has ~~spoke~~ *spoken*. Then, even if you wish to remain silent, you will be forced to repeat the last words you have ~~herd~~ *heard*."

"Alas!" cried all the nymphs at once.

"Alas!" cried Echo. She could say nothing else, even though she longed to beg Hera's ~~foregiveness~~ *forgiveness*. She could no longer speak to her sisters but was compelled to repeat what they said, ~~wether~~ *whether* she wanted to or not.

Error Summary

Language Usage	2
Punctuation:	
Apostrophe	1
Comma	1
Quotation Mark	4
Spelling	4

THURSDAY　　　　　　　　　　　　　　　Week 4

Echo left for the high slopes of mount helicon to live by her self. One day, a young man named Narcissus became lost in the woods. He ~~were~~ *was* so ~~hansom~~ *handsome* that Echo fell in love with him ~~immediate~~ *immediately*. Narcissus did not return her love. Instead he saw his own reflection in a pond and fell in love with it. As he ~~tries~~ *tried* to embrace ~~its~~ *his* own image, he ~~falls~~ *fell* into the water and ~~drownd~~ *drowned*. Heartbroken, Echo wept for Narcissus until she wasted away. Even though Echo was gone the power of Hera's curse continued. To this day, Echo's voice haunt's rocky hills, caves, and lofty halls that voice still ~~repetes~~ *repeats* the words it hears, ~~ansering~~ *answering* when someone else calls.

Error Summary

Capitalization	3
Language Usage	5
Punctuation:	
Apostrophe	3
Comma	2
Period	1
Spelling	5

Name _____

WEDNESDAY   Week 4

- adverbs
- verbs
- dialogue

The frightend Echo simply nodded. Hera continued to proclaim angry, The gift that you have used to trick me shall be yours no longer! From this moment on you will not be able to speak until someone else has spoke. Then, even if you wish to remain silent, you will be forced to repeat the last words you have herd.

"Alas!" cried all the nymphs at once.

Alas! cried Echo. She could say nothing else, even though she longed to beg Heras foregiveness. She could no longer speak to her sisters but was compelled to repeat what they said, wether she wanted to or not.

THURSDAY   Week 4

- adverbs
- verbs
- possessives

Echo left for the high slopes of mount helicon to live by her self. One day, a young man named Narcissus became lost in the woods. He were so hansom that Echo fell in love with him immediate. Narcissus did not return her love. Instead he saw his own reflection in a pond and fell in love with it. As he tries to embrace its own image, he falls into the water and drownd. Heartbroken, Echo wept for Narcissus until she wasted away. Even though Echo was gone the power of Heras curse continued. To this day, Echos voice haunt's rocky hills, caves, and lofty halls, that voice still repetes the words it hears, ansering when someone else calls.

MONDAY   Week 5

Sweet Insects

Honeybees come in different sizes and ~~got~~ (have) slightly

different ~~characsisticks~~ (characteristics). For example, the bees of one

species (named <u>Apis florea</u>) ~~builds~~ (build) their nests in trees. This

species ~~are~~ (is) found in central asia. The giant honeybee (<u>Apis</u>

<u>dorsata</u>), which is found in india, indonesia, and parts of

china, can build ~~honeycomes~~ (honeycombs) that are more than nine feet

in ~~diammeter~~ (diameter). another type of honeybee is the Eastern

honeybee, or <u>Apis indica</u>, which ~~beekeeppers~~ (beekeepers) in parts of

Asia raise. Probably the ~~more~~ (most) ~~familar~~ (familiar) species of all is the

domestic honeybee, or <u>Apis mellifera</u>.

Error Summary

Capitalization   6
Language Usage   4
Punctuation:
    Underlined Words 8
Spelling   5

TUESDAY   Week 5

the domestic honeybee is about half ~~a~~ (an) inch in ~~lenth~~ (length).

Although there is some variation. There ~~is~~ (are) short, stiff hairs

on the bee's head and thorax, which is the middle of the body.

The bee has two large compound eyes and three simple eyes.

Which are on top of its head. ~~Dummestic~~ (Domestic) honeybees have

~~exellent~~ (excellent) eyesight. They also have two antennae that ~~detects~~ (detect)

~~oder~~ (odor). Which is important ~~cuz~~ (because) bees need to locate ~~pollin~~ (pollen).

Although the four honeybee ~~speecies~~ (species) are somewhat

different, they ~~has~~ (have) some things in common. First, they all

make ~~honie~~ (honey). Second, they are all social insects and work

together as a group.

Error Summary

Capitalization   4
Language Usage   4
Punctuation:
    Comma   5
    Period   1
Spelling   8

Name _____

Sweet Insects

Honeybees come in different sizes and got slightly different characteristicks. For example, the bees of one species (named Apis florea) builds their nests in trees. This species are found in central asia. The giant honeybee (Apis dorsata), which is found in india, indonesia, and parts of china, can build honeycomes that are more than nine feet in diammeter. another type of honeybee is the Eastern honeybee, or Apis indica, which beekeeppers in parts of Asia raise. Probably the more familar species of all is the domestic honeybee, or Apis mellifera.

- scientific names
- geographic regions
- verbs

the domestic honeybee is about half a inch in lenth. Although there is some variation. There is short stiff hairs on the bee's head and thorax, which is the middle of the body. The bee has two large compound eyes and three simple eyes. Which are on top of its head. Dummestic honeybees have exellent eyesight. They also have two antennae that detects oder. Which is important cuz bees need to locate pollin

Although the four honeybee speecies are somewhat different, they has some things in common. First, they all make honie. Second they are all social insects and work together as a group.

- commas
- incomplete sentences
- verbs

WEDNESDAY　　　　　　　　　　　　Week 5

Honeybees communicate with each other through a
pattern
~~patern~~ of movement. They can tell about the location, distance,
size, and quality of a food source in the area, the message
helps other bees find the same food source.

　　A honeybee colony ~~colonny~~ has three classes, or castes:
drones, workers, and queens. All of the drones are male.
The workers are female, but are smaller than ~~then~~ the queens.
Both the workers and the queens lay ~~lays~~ eggs; however, only
the queens' eggs get fertilized. Drone's live in the colony for
only a brief ~~breef~~ season. Their only purpose ~~perpose~~ in the colony is to
fertilize
~~fertulize~~ the queens' eggs.

Error Summary

Capitalization	1
Language Usage	2
Punctuation:	
Apostrophe	2
Comma	4
Period	1
Spelling	5

THURSDAY　　　　　　　　　　　　Week 5

cycle
　　The honeybee's life ~~sikel~~ has four stages. It takes about
three days for the eggs to hatch. The larvae, also called
grubs, remain in their honeycomb cells. The worker bees
liquid
feed the grubs a thick, milky ~~liguid~~ called royal jelly, Which
is produced from glands in the worker bees' heads. About a
transform
week later, the grubs ~~transforum~~ into pupae. Two to three
their
weeks later, the bees emerge from ~~they're~~ cells. Queens are
emerge
the first to ~~emerje~~, followed by the workers and then the
drones
~~droans~~. once the queens emerge, they fight among ~~theirselves~~ themselves
survives　　　　　　　　then
until only one ~~servives~~. The new queen ~~than~~ attacks the old
forced
queen, which is ~~forst~~ to leave the nest.

Error Summary

Capitalization	2
Language Usage	2
Punctuation:	
Apostrophe	1
Comma	5
Spelling	8

Name _____

WEDNESDAY   Week 5

Honeybees communicate with each other through a patern of movement. They can tell about the location distance size and quality of a food source in the area, the message helps other bees find the same food source.

A honeybee colonny has three classes, or castes: drones, workers, and queens. All of the drones are male. The workers are female, but are smaller then the queens. Both the workers and the queens lays eggs; however, only the queens' eggs get fertilized. Drone's live in the colony for only a breef season. Their only perpose in the colony is to fertulize the queens eggs.

- commas
- apostrophes
- run-on sentences

THURSDAY   Week 5

The honeybee's life sikel has four stages. It takes about three days for the eggs to hatch. The larvae also called grubs remain in their honeycomb cells. The worker bees feed the grubs a thick milky liguid called royal jelly. Which is produced from glands in the worker bees heads. About a week later, the grubs transforum into pupae. Two to three weeks later, the bees emerge from they're cells. Queens are the first to emerje, followed by the workers and then the droans. once the queens emerge they fight among theirselves until only one servives. The new queen than attacks the old queen, which is forst to leave the nest.

- run-on sentences
- incomplete sentences
- commas

MONDAY   Week 6

Leaving Ireland

    Life had been ~~extremly~~ *extremely* hard for the O'Donnell Family for some time now. Two years ago, the ~~potatos~~ *potatoes* suddenly rotted in the ~~feilds~~ *fields*. Now, in 1847, the situation was even ~~worst~~ *worse*. It looked as if this year's crop also would be ~~effected~~ *affected*.

    Twelve-year-old Danny was helping his Parents harvest other ~~vegtables~~ *vegetables* from the fields, but they had not planted much besides potatoes they ~~bearly~~ *barely* had enough food to last the rest of the ~~weak~~ *week*.

    "Danny," said his father, "why don't you take Spot to the lake and see if you can catch a fish for tonight's supper?"

Error Summary

Capitalization	3
Language Usage	2
Punctuation:	
Apostrophe	3
Hyphen	2
Period	2
Question Mark	1
Quotation Mark	4
Spelling	6

TUESDAY   Week 6

    A stranger watching danny and his dog would think they didn't have a care in the world. That stranger would be so wrong, though. Danny was under ~~presher~~ *pressure* to catch a fish that day. If he didn't, his family would go hungry.

    As soon as Danny was out of earshot, Mr. O'Donnell took his wife's hand. "Fiona," he said, "I think we should sell the farm. That would give us enough money to ~~sale~~ *sail* to america. We'll ~~starv~~ *starve* if we stay here."

    "You're right, Patrick," said Fiona. "How many of our neighbors have ~~allready~~ *already* starved to ~~deth~~ *death*? This ~~fammin~~ *famine* has taken a terrible ~~tole~~ *toll*."

Error Summary

Capitalization	3
Punctuation:	
Apostrophe	2
Period	2
Question Mark	1
Quotation Mark	8
Spelling	7

Name _____

MONDAY   Week 6

Leaving Ireland

Life had been extremly hard for the O'Donnell Family for some time now. Two years ago, the potatos suddenly rotted in the feilds. Now, in 1847, the situation was even worst. It looked as if this years crop also would be effected

Twelve year old Danny was helping his Parents harvest other vegtables from the fields, but they had not planted much besides potatoes they bearly had enough food to last the rest of the weak.

Danny, said his father, why dont you take Spot to the lake and see if you can catch a fish for tonights supper

- apostrophes
- hyphens
- run-on sentences
- dialogue

TUESDAY   Week 6

A stranger watching danny and his dog would think they didn't have a care in the world. That stranger would be so wrong, though. Danny was under presher to catch a fish that day. If he didnt, his family would go hungry

as soon as Danny was out of earshot, Mr O'Donnell took his wifes hand. Fiona, he said, I think we should sell the farm. That would give us enough money to sale to america. We'll starv if we stay here.

You're right, Patrick, said Fiona. How many of our neighbors have allready starved to deth. This fammin has taken a terrible tole.

- run-on sentences
- apostrophes
- dialogue

WEDNESDAY　　　　　　　　　　　　　　Week 6

"It *pains* me to say it, Fiona," said Patrick, "but I'm afraid the british are either unwilling or *unable* to help us. There are many irish like us in boston. let's go there."

Five weeks later, early in the morning on the *appointed* day, the O'Donnell *family* stood at dock number 7 with their bags and with their dog, spot. They waited patiently until the gangplank was lowered to the dock. Along with the other passengers, they climbed on *board*. The *wealthy* passengers headed for their cabins. the poor ones, like the O'Donnells, headed for the steerage section in the deepest part of the ship.

Error Summary

Capitalization	6
Punctuation:	
Apostrophe	1
Period	2
Quotation Mark	4
Spelling	6

THURSDAY　　　　　　　　　　　　　　Week 6

After they got settled, Danny and his parents went back up on deck. Mr. and mrs. O'Donnell talked with the captain, who told them about *opportunities* in America.

"There's land for the taking," he declared.

"I've heard the same thing, captain," said Danny's father. "I'll be first in line when they hand out the land deeds."

Danny's mother agreed. "We've always been farmers. I don't think we'll stay in the city for long."

Danny didn't say it aloud, but he thought it might be better to try something new. Life in Boston was more *attractive* to him *than* life on a farm.

Error Summary

Capitalization	2
Language Usage	1
Punctuation:	
Apostrophe	3
Comma	4
Period	2
Quotation Mark	4
Spelling	2

Name _____

WEDNESDAY   Week 6

It panes me to say it, Fiona, said Patrick, but I'm afraid the british are either unwilling or unnable to help us. There are many irish like us in boston, lets go there.

Five weeks later, early in the morning on the apointed day, the O'Donnell fammily stood at dock number 7 with their bags and with their dog, spot. They waited patiently until the gangplank was lowered to the dock. Along with the other passengers, they climbed on bored. The welthy passengers headed for their cabins, the poor ones, like the O'Donnells, headed for the steerage section in the deepest part of the ship.

- dialogue
- nationalities
- run-on sentences

THURSDAY   Week 6

After they got settled Danny and his parents went back up on deck. Mr and mrs O'Donnell talked with the captain who told them about oppurtunities in America.

"There's land for the taking he declared.

"Ive heard the same thing, captain," said Danny's father. I'll be first in line when they hand out the land deeds.

Dannys mother agreed. "We've always been farmers. I don't think we'll stay in the city for long.

Danny didnt say it aloud but he thought it might be better to try something new. Life in Boston was more atractive to him then life on a farm.

- personal names
- apostrophes
- dialogue

MONDAY   Week 7

The King's Cupcakes

whose
Once there was a king ~~who's~~ happiness was complete

except for one thing: No one in his kingdom could make
pumpkin   satisfy   haven't   tasty
~~punkin~~ cupcakes to ~~satissfy~~ him. "I ~~hav'ent~~ had a ~~tastey~~
pumpkin
~~pumkin~~ cupcake since I was a prince," declared the king.

For some time, this king had been thinking about getting
married "   "   "   marry
~~marreyed~~. I have an idea," said the king. "I will ~~mary~~ a woman
                                               search
who can make pumpkin cupcakes!" He began his ~~serch~~. He
                                  kingdom
first went to Apple Hill, the ~~kingdum~~ to the north. There, he

saw queen Appelonia, who was as kind as she was beautiful.

"Can you make pumpkin cupcakes?" he asked.

Error Summary

Capitalization	1
Punctuation:	
Comma	2
Quotation Mark	6
Spelling	10

TUESDAY   Week 7

"   replied "
"No," she ~~replyed~~, but I can make wonderful apple pies."
"   responded "
"That won't do," the king ~~reponded~~. "I want a ~~Q~~ueen who

can make pumpkin cupcakes. Even so, I enjoyed meeting you."

Next, he went to Terra Incognita, the kingdom to the

south, to see Queen Malicious. She was not as kind as she

was beautiful, but the king asked, "Can you make cupcakes?"
"   "   spicy
"No," she said, "but my ~~spicey~~ curry sauce is tasty."

"I like curry, but I like cupcakes more," the king said.

Next, the king went to Zamboni, the kingdom to the

~~E~~ast, to see Queen Plain Jane, who was not as beautiful as

she was kind.

Error Summary

Capitalization	2
Punctuation:	
Apostrophe	1
Comma	4
Quotation Mark	11
Spelling	3

Name _____

The King's Cupcakes

Once there was a king who's happiness was complete except for one thing: No one in his kingdom could make punkin cupcakes to satissfy him. "I hav'ent had a tastey pumkin cupcake since I was a prince, declared the king.

For some time this king had been thinking about getting marreyed. I have an idea, said the king. I will mary a woman who can make pumpkin cupcakes! He began his serch. He first went to Apple Hill the kingdum to the north. There, he saw queen Appelonia, who was as kind as she was beautiful. "Can you make pumpkin cupcakes? he asked.

- pronouns
- personal names
- titles of people
- dialogue

No she replyed, but I can make wonderful apple pies."

That wont do," the king reponded. I want a Queen who can make pumpkin cupcakes. Even so, I enjoyed meeting you."

Next he went to Terra Incognita, the kingdom to the south to see Queen Malicious. She was not as kind as she was beautiful, but the king asked, "Can you make cupcakes?

No, she said, but my spicey curry sauce is tasty.

"I like curry, but I like cupcakes more, the king said.

Next, the king went to Zamboni, the kingdom to the East, to see Queen Plain Jane who was not as beautiful as she was kind.

- commas
- apostrophes
- dialogue

WEDNESDAY   Week 7

Before he could say a word, she ~~ask~~ asked "Can you play the bassoon? I won't marry a man who can't play the bassoon."

"I cannot," ~~says~~ said the king, "but I can play the xylophone."

"Sorry," she said. "That won't do."

The king went home alone. There, the prime ~~minestir~~ minister advised him to find a queen, even if she wasn't ideal. So the king went to see Queen Appelonia again, only to find that she ~~have~~ had married the owner of an apple ~~orchurd~~ orchard and opened a ~~bakkry~~ bakery. He returned to Terra Incognita but ~~finds~~ found that a ~~draggon~~ dragon had ~~seezed~~ seized Queen Malicious for her spicy sauce ~~recepie~~ recipe, which he needed for his ~~firey~~ fiery breath.

Error Summary

Language Usage	4
Punctuation:	
Apostrophe	3
Comma	2
Quotation Mark	10
Spelling	7

THURSDAY   Week 7

In the end, the king proposed to queen plain jane of zamboni. She ~~aggreed~~ agreed to marry him because he was such a good king. A year later, though, they had an ~~awfull~~ awful argument.

"Why can't you make pumpkin cupcakes?" he yelled.

"Hey, why can't you play the bassoon?" she shouted back.

They ~~did'nt~~ didn't speak to each other all that day. Soon, however, they realized that they had been foolish. Eventually, the king learned to make pumpkin cupcakes ~~hisself~~ himself, and the queen learned to play the bassoon. The King then issued this statement to the people of his kingdom: "If you want something done, learn to do it yourself."

Error Summary

Capitalization	6
Language Usage	1
Punctuation:	
Comma	4
Question Mark	1
Quotation Mark	3
Spelling	3

Name _____

WEDNESDAY　　　　　　　　　　　　　　　Week 7

Before he could say a word, she ask Can you play the bassoon? I won't marry a man who cant play the bassoon.

I cannot says the king, but I can play the xylophone.

Sorry, she said. That wont do.

The king went home alone. There, the prime minestir advised him to find a queen, even if she wasnt ideal. So the king went to see Queen Appelonia again, only to find that she have married the owner of an apple orchurd and opened a bakkry. He returned to Terra Incognita but finds that a draggon had seezed Queen Malicious for her spicy sauce recepie, which he needed for his firey breath.

WATCH FOR

• verbs
• dialogue
• apostrophes

THURSDAY　　　　　　　　　　　　　　　Week 7

In the end, the king proposed to queen plain jane of zamboni. She aggreed to marry him because he was such a good king. A year later, though, they had an awfull argument.

"Why can't you make pumpkin cupcakes? he yelled.

"Hey why can't you play the bassoon She shouted back.

They did'nt speak to each other all that day. Soon however they realized that they had been foolish. Eventually, the king learned to make pumpkin cupcakes hisself, and the queen learned to play the bassoon. The King then issued this statement to the people of his kingdom: "If you want something done learn to do it yourself.

WATCH FOR

• personal names
• titles of people
• apostrophes
• dialogue

MONDAY   Week 8

A Natural Home

Do you like frogs, lizards, and snakes? If so, you

might enjoy having a vivarium, an enclosed space for keeping

organisms
organisims to observe. A vivarium is a setting, that resembles ressembles

the natural surroundings of the organisms you put in it. By

particular
using rocks, soil, and water in partiklar ways, you can create

environment
an enviurnment like that of a rainforest or a desert.

When you make a vivarium, you need to choose chuze plants

compatible
and animals that are compatable with that environment. A

obviously
vivarium that has desert plants and rainforest animals obviosly

successful
wouldn't be very sucesful.

Error Summary

Punctuation:

Apostrophe	1
Comma	6
Period	1
Question Mark	1
Spelling	8

TUESDAY   Week 8

suited
Many different kinds of animals are sooted to

lizards
vivariums. Frogs, snakes, and lizzards are good choices. Other

possibilities are
possibleties is salamanders, toads, turtles, spiders, newts, and

insects. Of course, you can include two or more different

is
animals. The main thing to remember are that one animal

must not think of the other animals as dinner!

You should also think about what to feed the plants

and animals in your vivarium. The plants might need fertilizer,

from time to time. The animals might need live food, such as

crickets
crickits, maggots, or mice. Many pet stores sell live food, but

separate
you can also raise live food in a seperete vivarium.

Error Summary

Capitalization	1
Language Usage	2

Punctuation:

Apostrophe	2
Comma	10
Period	1
Spelling	5

Name _____

A Natural Home

Do you like frogs lizards and snakes. If so, you might enjoy having a vivarium an enclosed space for keeping organisims to observe. A vivarium is a setting, that ressembles the natural surroundings of the organisms you put in it. By using rocks soil and water in partiklar ways, you can create an enviurnment like that of a rainforest or a desert.

When you make a vivarium, you need to chuze plants and animals that are compatable with that environment A vivarium that has desert plants and rainforest animals obviosly wouldnt be very sucesful.

- commas
- end punctuation

Many different kinds of animals are sooted to vivariums. Frogs, snakes and lizzards are good choices. Other possibleties is salamanders toads turtles spiders newts and insects. Of course you can include two or more different animals. The main thing to remember are that one animal must not think of the other animals as dinner!

You should also think about what to feed the plant's and animal's in your vivarium. The plants might need fertilizer. From time to time. The animals might need live food, such as crickits maggots or mice. Many pet stores sell live food but you can also raise live food in a seperete vivarium.

- commas
- apostrophes
- verbs
- incomplete sentences

WEDNESDAY   Week 8

       temperature
The ~~tempature~~ inside a vivarium must be ~~apropriate~~ appropriate for
the plants and animals that live in it. Therefore, all of the
organisms
~~organizms~~ should have the same requirements. For example,
    wouldn't
it ~~would'nt~~ be good to combine plants that need a warm
environment with animals that need a cool environment.

       desert
Let's say you want to set up a vivarium with a ~~dessert~~
        an
environment. Start with a aquarium. Add a layer of gravel
and sand. Place a flat rock in the sand. it gives the animals
   themselves
a place to sun ~~themselfs~~. Add a small branch for shade. it
gives the animals a place to hide. Use a heat lamp to achieve
          degrees
the proper Temperature—usually 85 to 90 ~~degrese~~ Fahrenheit.

Error Summary

Capitalization	3
Language Usage	1
Punctuation:	
Apostrophe	1
Period	2
Spelling	7

THURSDAY   Week 8

A vivarium can also have a Damp Forest environment.
salamanders and many kinds of frogs can thrive there. The
best plants for this type of vivarium are moss, ivy, and small
      aquarium
houseplant's. Begin with an ~~acquarium~~. Line the bottom with
          drainage
about two inches of gravel. this will provide ~~drainege~~. Add
three to four inches of sterilized topsoil, which you can
purchase
~~purchus~~ from a plant nursery. Then add a thin ~~layar~~ layer of peat
moss. this will help keep moisture in the vivarium. Use a desk
lamp for light and heat. don't forget to provide water. After
observing the organisms every day for a few months, you will
    behave
learn how they ~~beehave~~ in a natural setting.

Error Summary

Capitalization	6
Punctuation:	
Apostrophe	2
Comma	3
Period	4
Spelling	5

Name _____

WEDNESDAY   Week 8

The tempature inside a vivarium must be apropriate for the plants and animals that live in it. Therefore, all of the organizms should have the same requirements. For example, it would'nt be good to combine plants that need a warm environment with animals that need a cool environment.

Lets say you want to set up a vivarium with a dessert environment. Start with a aquarium. Add a layer of gravel and sand. Place a flat rock in the sand, it gives the animals a place to sun themselfs. Add a small branch for shade, it gives the animals a place to hide. Use a heat lamp to achieve the proper Temperature—usually 85 to 90 degrese Fahrenheit.

- apostrophes
- run-on sentences

THURSDAY   Week 8

A vivarium can also have a Damp Forest environment, salamanders and many kinds of frogs can thrive there. The best plants for this type of vivarium are moss ivy and small houseplant's. Begin with an acquarium. Line the bottom with about two inches of gravel, this will provide drainege. Add three to four inches of sterilized topsoil which you can purchus from a plant nursery. Then add a thin layar of peat moss, this will help keep moisture in the vivarium. Use a desk lamp for light and heat, dont forget to provide water. After observing the organisms every day for a few months, you will learn how they beehave in a natural setting.

- run-on sentences
- commas

MONDAY	Week 9

Student Elections

Vinnie and Eddie were in the same seventh-grade class.
They had been best ~~freinds~~ *friends* since second grade, and they
agreed on nearly everything—until that one day in november.
Walking down the hall, a strange ~~thing~~ *they saw something—that* caught their attention.
Some kids were vandalizing the paintings in the art display
case. One of those kids Jason Walker had been in Eddies
class last year. Jason noticed that Eddie recognized him, and
he stared aggressively at Eddie.

As they continued down the hall, Vinnie whispered come
on, Eddie. Lets report those guys to the ~~principle~~ *principal*.

Error Summary

Capitalization	2
Punctuation:	
Apostrophe	2
Comma	3
Hyphen	1
Quotation Mark	2
Sentence Structure	1
Spelling	2

TUESDAY	Week 9

"I cant Vinnie," said Eddie. I know that guy, and hes
tough. Besides, I don't have time. I have to go home and
work on my ~~campain~~ *campaign*. Did you forget that Im running for
student-body president? The ~~ellection~~ *election* is next week.

"I can't believe you wont back me up on this, Eddie"
said Vinnie.

"Sorry Vinnie. I have to get home" Eddie replied.

As Eddie hurried home, Vinnie went to the principals
office to report the vandalism. Later that afternoon, he
talked with his Mother about what had ~~happenned~~ *happened*. She
shared Vinnies disappointment in Eddie.

Error Summary

Capitalization	1
Punctuation:	
Apostrophe	6
Comma	5
Question Mark	1
Quotation Mark	2
Spelling	3

Name _____

- hyphens
- dangling modifiers
- apostrophes
- dialogue

Student Elections

Vinnie and Eddie were in the same seventh grade class. They had been best freinds since second grade, and they agreed on nearly everything—until that one day in november. Walking down the hall, a strange thing caught their attention. Some kids were vandalizing the paintings in the art display case. One of those kids Jason Walker had been in Eddies class last year. Jason noticed that Eddie recognized him, and he stared aggressively at Eddie.

As they continued down the hall, Vinnie whispered come on, Eddie. Lets report those guys to the principle.

- commas
- apostrophes
- end punctuation
- dialogue

"I cant Vinnie," said Eddie. I know that guy, and hes tough. Besides, I don't have time. I have to go home and work on my campain. Did you forget that Im running for student-body president. The ellection is next week.

"I can't believe you wont back me up on this, Eddie" said Vinnie.

"Sorry Vinnie. I have to get home" Eddie replied.

As Eddie hurried home, Vinnie went to the principals office to report the vandalism. Later that afternoon he talked with his Mother about what had happened. She shared Vinnies disappointment in Eddie.

WEDNESDAY   Week 9

That night, vinnie had a hard time getting to sleep. He kept thinking about how ~~dissapointed~~ disappointed he was in his friend. He also began to wonder if Eddie would really make a good president. ~~Untill~~ Until now, Vinnie had supported his friend. Now he was beginning to question things. If Eddie could ~~ignoar~~ ignore vandalism, then perhaps his character wasn't so ~~sollid~~ solid.

The next morning, as the two friends were walking to school, eddie announced, "I've been giving it some thought and have decided to withdraw from the election. What kind of president would I be if I couldn't even report those guys yesterday? I think you should run, Vinnie."

Error Summary

Capitalization	2
Punctuation:	
Apostrophe	3
Comma	3
Question Mark	1
Quotation Mark	1
Spelling	4

THURSDAY   Week 9

Vinnie thought about his friend's suggestion all day. That evening, he ~~talks~~ talked it over with his parents.

"So, have you decided to run?" asked his mother.

"I ~~gues~~ guess I have," replied Vinnie. "You know, mom, I actually felt scared when I saw those guys vandalizing the paintings. No one knows what they might do next. I ~~should'nt~~ shouldn't have to feel afraid at school, and neither should ~~nobody~~ anybody else. Students should be able to report crimes and ~~violince~~ violence at school. That will be the main point of my ~~campagn~~ campaign."

Vinnie's Dad ~~says~~ said, "Great idea! I'll help you make some posters. I think you just might win this election."

Error Summary

Capitalization	2
Language Usage	3
Punctuation:	
Apostrophe	2
Comma	1
Question Mark	1
Quotation Mark	3
Spelling	4

Name _____

WEDNESDAY	Week 9

     That night, vinnie had a hard time getting to sleep. He kept thinking about how dissapointed he was in his friend. He also began to wonder if Eddie would really make a good president. Untill now, Vinnie had supported his friend. Now he was beginning to question things. If Eddie could ignoar vandalism then perhaps his character wasnt so sollid.

     The next morning, as the two friends were walking to school, eddie announced "Ive been giving it some thought and have decided to withdraw from the election. What kind of president would I be if I couldnt even report those guys yesterday. I think you should run Vinnie.

- commas
- apostrophes
- end punctuation
- dialogue

THURSDAY	Week 9

     Vinnie thought about his friends suggestion all day. That evening, he talks it over with his parents.

     "So, have you decided to run" asked his mother.

     "I gues I have" replied Vinnie. You know, mom, I actually felt scared when I saw those guys vandalizing the paintings. No one knows what they might do next. I should'nt have to feel afraid at school, and neither should nobody else. Students should be able to report crimes and violince at school. That will be the main point of my campagn."

     Vinnies Dad says, Great idea! I'll help you make some posters. I think you just might win this election.

- verbs
- end punctuation
- double negatives
- dialogue

MONDAY   **Week 10**

The Triangle Shirtwaist Factory Fire

March 25 1911, started out as an ordinary spring saturday in new york city. Five hundred workers mostly young women reported to work at the ten-story building at the corner of washington place and Greene street. They headed upstairs to the top three floors, where the triangle waist company manufactured shirtwaists, a type of womens blouse

height

that was the ~~hite~~ of fashion at the time. Tragically, 146 of

would

those workers ~~wood~~ never return home. the fire that would start just before closing time would cost them their lives.

than   *were*

more ~~then~~ four-tenths of the victims ~~was~~ teenagers.

Error Summary

Capitalization	12
Language Usage	2
Punctuation:	
Apostrophe	1
Comma	3
Hyphen	2
Spelling	2

TUESDAY   **Week 10**

a fire broke out on the eighth floor of the building

was

at about 440 in the afternoon. The eighth floor ~~were~~ where

forty

~~fourty~~ workers all men cut fabric at long wooden tables.

wasted

Although the skilled workers ~~waisted~~ little fabric, they always

produced   *thrown*

~~produiced~~ some scraps. these scraps were ~~throne~~ into bins

dealer

under the tables. Roughly every two months, a rag ~~deeler~~

scraps   *sold*

removed about a ton of ~~scrapes~~ and ~~sells~~ them back to cotton mills that made new cloth from them. The last pickup

meant

had been in january which ~~means~~ of course that the bins beneath the wooden tables held about a ton of scraps. These

were

scraps ~~was~~ not the only flammable materials in the room.

Error Summary

Capitalization	3
Language Usage	4
Punctuation:	
Colon	1
Comma	5
Hyphen	1
Spelling	6

Name _____

MONDAY   Week 10

- place names
- company names
- commas
- hyphens

The Triangle Shirtwaist Factory Fire

March 25 1911, started out as an ordinary spring saturday in new york city. Five hundred workers mostly young women reported to work at the ten story building at the corner of washington place and Greene street. They headed upstairs to the top three floors, where the triangle waist company manufactured shirtwaists, a type of womens blouse that was the hite of fashion at the time. Tragically, 146 of those workers wood never return home. the fire that would start just before closing time would cost them their lives. more then four tenths of the victims was teenagers.

TUESDAY   Week 10

- commas
- time
- verbs

a fire broke out on the eighth floor of the building at about 440 in the afternoon. The eighth floor were where fourty workers all men cut fabric at long wooden tables. Although the skilled workers waisted little fabric, they always produiced some scraps. these scraps were throne into bins under the tables. Roughly every two-months, a rag deelar removed about a ton of scrapes and sells them back to cotton mills that made new cloth from them. The last pickup had been in january which means of course that the bins beneath the wooden tables held about a ton of scraps. These scraps was not the only flammable materials in the room.

WEDNESDAY   Week 10

On a typical workday, cutters on the eighth floor spread 120 layers of sheer, lightweight ~~fabbrick~~ fabric on their tables. the layers were separated with sheets of ~~tishue~~ tissue paper. The fabric, like the tissue paper, ~~were~~ was as ~~flammible~~ flammable as gasoline. About a hundred ~~woman~~ women worked on that floor. Paper patterns hung from lengths of string over the tables. on the ~~nineth~~ ninth floor, nearly 300 women were ~~sewing~~ sewing garments. Stored nearby ~~was~~ were cans of highly flammable oil used to make the sewing machines run ~~smoothley~~ smoothly. The Tenth Floor was where the ~~finnished~~ finished garments ~~was~~ were inspected, packaged, and shipped.

Error Summary

Capitalization	4
Language Usage	4
Punctuation:	
Comma	5
Period	2
Spelling	7

THURSDAY   Week 10

No one knows for sure what ~~start~~ started the fire. It ~~begin~~ began on the eighth floor in the scraps that were stored in the bins. A live ash from a ~~cigaratte~~ cigarette may ~~had~~ have been the cause. In any case, the fire spread ~~quick~~ quickly to the ninth floor. Because the stairway doors were locked, the women ~~their~~ there didn't have ~~no~~ any way to escape. Panicked workers crowded onto the fire escape, which ~~collapses~~ collapsed from too much ~~wait~~ weight. Others jumped from windows to the pavement ninety-five feet below. Nearly all who died were women between fourteen and twenty-three years old who had recently ~~imigrated~~ immigrated from italy or russia. It was the ~~worse~~ worst workplace disaster the country had ever ~~saw~~ seen.

Error Summary

Capitalization	2
Language Usage	8
Punctuation:	
Hyphen	2
Period	1
Spelling	4

Name _____

WEDNESDAY   Week 10

- commas
- run-on sentences

On a typical workday, cutters on the eighth floor spread 120 layers of sheer lightweight fabbrick on their tables the layers were separated with sheets of tishue paper. The fabric like the tissue paper were as flammible as gasoline. About a hundred woman worked on that floor Paper patterns hung from lengths of string over the tables. on the nineth floor, nearly 300 women were sowing garments. Stored nearby was cans of highly flammable oil used to make the sewing machines run smoothley. The Tenth Floor was where the finnished garments was inspected packaged and shipped.

THURSDAY   Week 10

- place names
- verbs
- adverbs
- words that compare

No one knows for sure what start the fire. It begin on the eighth floor in the scraps that were stored in the bins. A live ash from a cigaratte may had been the cause. In any case, the fire spread quick to the ninth floor. Because the stairway doors were locked, the women their didn't have no way to escape. Panicked workers crowded onto the fire escape, which collapses from too much wait. Others jumped from windows to the pavement ninety five feet below. Nearly all who died were women between fourteen and twenty three years old who had recently imigrated from italy or russia. It was the worse workplace disaster the country had ever saw

MONDAY   Week 11

The Snake Charmer

Scott's friends had come over to watch a tv program
about snakes; they all knew about Scott's intense interest
in the creepy ~~creatchers~~ creatures and pretended to be interested,
just to be ~~pollite~~ polite. Scott's most recent ~~edition~~ addition to his reptile
collection was a rare python. He had named her India, which
is where she came from.

Scott's ~~geusts~~ guests were dismayed when he brought india
into the living room. "Dont worry, said Scott. "Pythons are
really quite ~~harmlessly~~ harmless. Just don't make any sudden moves.
If a python is startled, it might attack."

Error Summary

Capitalization	4
Language Usage	1
Punctuation:	
Apostrophe	2
Comma	3
Period	1
Quotation Mark	3
Spelling	4

TUESDAY   Week 11

Scott placed the python on the floor, where she ~~curld~~ curled
up into a coil. Just then, Daniel dropped a ~~potatoe~~ potato chip on the
floor and bent over ~~quick~~ quickly to pick it up. what a mistake that
was! India, frightened by this sudden move, wrapped herself
around Daniels ~~waste~~ waist and didn't show ~~no~~ any signs of letting go.
Scotts ~~sootheing~~ soothing words did not seem to calm her down. Jane
thought the snake might ~~strangel~~ strangle Daniel; she reached for
the phone, called the paramedics, and asked for help.

Within minutes, Scott's living room was full of
firefighters, paramedics, sheriff's deputies, and animal-control
officers. Each one had a different ~~solusion~~ solution to the problem.

Error Summary

Capitalization	1
Language Usage	2
Punctuation:	
Apostrophe	2
Comma	10
Exclamation Point	1
Spelling	6

Name _____

MONDAY   Week 11

The Snake Charmer

Scott's friends had come over to watch a tv program about snakes, they all knew about Scott's intense interest in the creepy creatchers and pretended to be interested, just to be pollite. Scotts most recent edition to his reptile collection was a rare python. He had named her India which is where she came from.

Scott's geusts were dismayed when he brought india into the living room. "Dont worry said Scott. Pythons are really quite harmlessly. Just don't make any sudden moves. If a python is startled it might attack.

WATCH FOR

- commas
- apostrophes
- dialogue

TUESDAY   Week 11

Scott placed the python on the floor where she curld up into a coil. Just then Daniel dropped a potatoe chip on the floor and bent over quick to pick it up. what a mistake that was. India frightened by this sudden move wrapped herself around Daniels waste and didn't show no signs of letting go. Scotts sootheing words did not seem to calm her down. Jane thought the snake might strangel Daniel; she reached for the phone called the paramedics and asked for help.

Within minutes Scott's living room was full of firefighters paramedics sheriff's deputies and animal-control officers. Each one had a different solusion to the problem.

WATCH FOR

- commas
- end punctuation
- adverbs

WEDNESDAY   Week 11

One of the firefighter's said, "I think we'll have to cut off the snake's head."

"No way!" said Scott. "She's just scared; we can find a way to ~~persuede~~ *persuade* her to let go." Meanwhile, Daniel was fine.

They tried everything—from soft music to ice packs—but nothing seemed to work. Suddenly, one of the paramedics had an idea. "I read that snakes are ~~sensative~~ *sensitive* to odors. I think we should try smelling salts," she suggested.

Scott was willing to try any thing, as long as it didn't hurt India, so the paramedic broke open an ammonia capsule and held it close to India's head.

Error Summary

Capitalization	1
Punctuation:	
Apostrophe	4
Comma	3
Period	2
Quotation Mark	4
Spelling	3

THURSDAY   Week 11

India ~~relaxes~~ *relaxed* immediately, and Scott unwound her from Daniel's waist. Everyone breathed a sigh of ~~releif~~ *relief* as Scott ~~takes~~ *took* India back to her ~~enclozure~~ *enclosure*. When he returned to the room, the sheriff's deputies and the others were just leaving.

Scott thanked them for their help; then he turned to his guests and said, "We missed most of the show, but we can still watch the last part," as he ~~fliped~~ *flipped* on the TV. His guests groaned, having seen enough of snakes for a while.

"Snakes are very sensitive to odors; they are also frightened by sudden movements," the narrator was saying. Scott ~~laught quiet~~ *laughed quietly* and turned off the TV.

Error Summary

Capitalization	2
Language Usage	3
Punctuation:	
Apostrophe	2
Comma	5
Period	2
Quotation Mark	1
Spelling	4

Name _____

| WEDNESDAY | Week 11 |

- commas
- apostrophes
- dialogue
- compound words

One of the firefighter's said I think we'll have to cut off the snakes head."

"No way!" said Scott. She's just scared, we can find a way to persuede her to let go" Meanwhile, Daniel was fine.

They tried everything—from soft music to ice packs—but nothing seemed to work. Suddenly one of the paramedics had an idea. I read that snakes are sensative to odors. I think we should try smelling salts, she suggested.

Scott was willing to try any thing, as long as it didnt hurt India so the paramedic broke open an ammonia capsule and held it close to Indias head.

| THURSDAY | Week 11 |

- verbs
- apostrophes
- commas
- dialogue

India relaxes immediately, and Scott unwound her from Daniels' waist. Everyone breathed a sigh of releif as Scott takes India back to her enclozure. When he returned to the room the sheriffs deputies and the others were just leaving.

Scott thanked them for their help then he turned to his guests and said "We missed most of the show but we can still watch the last part" as he fliped on the TV. His guests groaned having seen enough of snakes for a while.

"Snakes are very sensitive to odors they are also frightened by sudden movements, the narrator was saying. Scott laught quiet and turned off the TV.

MONDAY   Week 12

A Sea That's Not a Sea

Despite its name, the Dead Sea is not really a sea; this landlocked Lake is about fifteen miles East of Jerusalem. Its water has such a high consentration *(concentration)* of minnerals *(minerals)* that colums *(columns)* of salt form and rise above the surface; these formations, according to some people, look like oddly shaped icebergs. The Dead Sea is the world's saltyest *(saltiest)* body of water. Normaly *(Normally)*, seawater has a salt content of 3.5 percent. By contrast, the water in the Dead Sea is 28 percent salt—eight times as salty as the ocean. It is even saltier than the Great Salt Lake in utah, which is six times as salty as ocean water.

Error Summary

Capitalization	4
Punctuation:	
Comma	3
Period	1
Spelling	5

TUESDAY   Week 12

The saltiness of the water is the reason that objects float so well in the lake. According to Rupert o Matthews, which *(who)* wrote the book The atlas of natural Wonders, ". . .it is far easier to swim or float here than in any other stretch of water." Can you imagine how it would feel to flaot *(float)* in this lake? You could even read a book as you floated along!

Indirectly, the dead sea gets its name from its salt kontent *(content)*. Can you guess why? The fact is, salt kills almost every form of life that is sweept *(swept)* into the Dead Sea. Very few organisms, such as certain kinds of bactirea *(bacteria)*, can live in this salty environment.

Error Summary

Capitalization	5
Language Usage	1
Punctuation:	
Ellipses	1
Period	1
Question Mark	2
Underlined Words	5
Spelling	4

Name _____

A Sea That's Not a Sea

Despite its name, the Dead Sea is not really a sea, this landlocked Lake is about fifteen miles East of Jerusalem. Its water has such a high consentration of minnerals that colums of salt form and rise above the surface; these formations, according to some people look like oddly shaped icebergs. The Dead Sea is the world's saltyest body of water. Normaly, seawater has a salt content of 3.5 percent. By contrast the water in the Dead Sea is 28 percent salt—eight times as salty as the ocean. It is even saltier than the Great Salt Lake in utah which is six times as salty as ocean water.

- run-on sentences
- commas
- place names

The saltiness of the water is the reason that objects float so well in the lake. According to Rupert o Matthews, which wrote the book The atlas of natural Wonders, "..it is far easier to swim or float here than in any other stretch of water." Can you imagine how it would feel to flaot in this lake. You could even read a book as you floated along!

Indirectly, the dead sea gets its name from its salt kontent. Can you guess why. The fact is, salt kills almost every form of life that is sweept into the Dead Sea. Very few organisms, such as certain kinds of bactirea, can live in this salty environment.

- pronouns
- personal names
- book titles
- end punctuation
- ellipses

WEDNESDAY   Week 12

These ~~extraordinery~~ *extraordinary*, single-celled organisms of the Halobacterium species thrive in warm water that ~~have~~ *has* high concentrations of salt. The bacteria ~~lives~~ *live* only in places such as the Great Salt Lake and the Dead sea. These purple organisms have a special light-sensitive protein that gathers sunlight—just as chlorophyll in green plants ~~collect~~ *collects* ~~sunlife~~ *sunlight*. They could not survive in a less saline environment.

The extreme saltiness of the Dead Sea is not its only ~~yuneek~~ *unique* feature. It also ~~claim~~ *claims* the ~~distinkshun~~ *distinction* of being the lowest body of water on the planet's surface, with an ~~ellavation~~ *elevation* of 1,300 feet below ~~see~~ *sea* level.

Error Summary

Capitalization	2
Language Usage	4
Punctuation:	
Apostrophe	1
Hyphen	2
Underlined Words	1
Spelling	6

THURSDAY   Week 12

Another ~~interresting~~ *interesting* fact about the Dead Sea is, that the concentration of salt changes ~~acording~~ *according* to depth. The water is much saltier in the deepest part's. That's because salt water is ~~densser~~ *denser* than fresh water. From the surface down to a depth of 130 feet, the salinity is about 300 parts per thousand. (In other words, every cup of water has nearly one-third cup of salt.) A 200-foot-thick layer below that has a salinity of about 332 parts per ~~thousend~~ *thousand*. The water is saltiest at a depth of more than 330 feet below the surface. It is so dense that it stays on the bottom. By now, you can understand why the dead sea is also called the salt sea.

Error Summary

Capitalization	4
Punctuation:	
Apostrophe	2
Comma	3
Hyphen	2
Parentheses	1
Spelling	4

Name _____

WEDNESDAY   Week 12

- hyphens
- scientific names
- verbs

These extraordinery, single celled organisms of the Halobacterium species thrive in warm water that have high concentrations of salt. The bacteria lives only in places such as the Great Salt Lake and the Dead sea. These purple organisms have a special light sensitive protein that gathers sunlight—just as chlorophyll in green plants collect sunlite. They could not survive in a less saline environment.

The extreme saltiness of the Dead Sea is not its only yuneek feature. It also claim the distinkshun of being the lowest body of water on the Planets surface, with an ellavation of 1,300 feet below see level.

THURSDAY   Week 12

- parentheses
- hyphens
- place names

Another interresting fact about the Dead Sea is, that the concentration of salt changes acording to depth. The water is much saltier in the deepest part's. Thats because salt water is densser than fresh water. From the surface down to a depth of 130 feet the salinity is about 300 parts per thousand. (In other words, every cup of water has nearly one third cup of salt. A 200 foot-thick layer below that has a salinity of about 332 parts per thousend. The water is saltiest at a depth of more than 330 feet below the surface. It is so dense that it stays on the bottom. By now you can understand why the dead sea is also called the salt sea.

MONDAY   Week 13

Error Summary

Capitalization	3
Language Usage	3
Punctuation:	
Comma	2
Hyphen	2
Period	1
Question Mark	1
Underlined Words	1
Spelling	6

Georges Méliès, Film Pioneer

One of the characters in the film <u>Hugo</u> is based on a real-life person named Georges Méliès (mehl-yes). This 2011 movie ~~portray~~ *portrays* him as ~~a~~ *an* old man. Who was Méliès and how did he become a film pioneer? georges méliès was a ~~majishun~~ *magician* who began working with film in the late 1890s. At that time, film ~~teknology~~ *technology* was in its ~~infintsy~~ *infancy*. Méliès studied the new ~~tekneeks~~ *techniques* being used by other film ~~pionnears~~ *pioneers*, including Louis and Auguste Lumière, whose inventions ~~brung~~ *brought* moving pictures to audiences, for the first time. Méliès ordered custom-made projectors and processing ~~equiptmint~~ *equipment*, and started to work.

TUESDAY   Week 13

Error Summary

Capitalization	2
Language Usage	2
Punctuation:	
Comma	6
Spelling	8

With his new equipment, Méliès began to make short, simple films. Soon, however, he ~~start~~ *started* to film the ~~majik~~ *magic* acts that ~~was~~ *were* being performed at the theater he ~~ownd~~ *owned* in paris, france. By 1896, he was producing his first "trick" films using special ~~uffecks~~ *effects* and multiple exposures to create ~~sertin~~ *certain* illusions. In his films, people and objects often seemed to transform ~~fissikly~~ *physically*, or they appeared and then ~~vannisht~~ *vanished* mysteriously. The effects were ~~quiet~~ *quite* entertaining. He also experimented with editing techniques that allowed him to make longer, more complex moving pictures. The ~~imajinative~~ *imaginative* movies that Méliès made, influenced the future of filmmaking.

Name _____

| MONDAY | Week 13 |

Georges Méliès, Film Pioneer

One of the characters in the film Hugo is based on a real life person named Georges Méliès (mehl-yes). This 2011 movie portray him as a old man. Who was Méliès and how did he become a film pioneer. georges méliès was a majishun who began working with film in the late 1890s. At that time, film teknology was in its infintsy. Méliès studied the new tekneeks being used by other film pionnears, including Louis and Auguste Lumière whose inventions brung moving pictures to audiences, for the first time. Méliès ordered custom made projectors and processing equiptmint. And started to work.

* hyphens
* movie titles
* end punctuation

| TUESDAY | Week 13 |

With his new equipment, Méliès began to make short simple films. Soon however he start to film the majik acts that was being performed at the theater he ownd in paris france. By 1896, he was producing his first "trick" films using special uffecks and multiple exposures to create sertin illusions. In his films, people and objects often seemed to transform fissikly, or they appeared and then vannisht mysteriously. The effects were quiet entertaining. He also experimented with editing techniques that allowed him to make longer more complex moving pictures. The imajinative movies that Méliès made, influenced the future of filmmaking.

* commas
* verbs
* place names

WEDNESDAY   Week 13

Other filmmakers were making single-shot films but
Méliès linked ~~nummerus~~ numerous shots together. In 1899, he released
the seven-minute film <u>Cinderella</u> which told the familiar ~~ferry~~ fairy
tale in 20 scenes. His best-known film was ~~relleased~~ released in 1902.
Titled <u>A Trip to the Moon</u> it was loosely based on two books
that were popular at the time. Those books were <u>From the</u>
<u>Earth to the Moon</u> by Jules Verne and <u>The First Men in the</u>
<u>Moon</u> by H. G. Wells. The film ran 14 minutes when ~~perjected~~ projected
at 16 frames per second, the usual speed at the time. Today,
movies are ~~typical~~ typically projected at 24 to 30 frames per second,
so the motion is smoother and ~~least choppy~~ less choppy.

Error Summary

Language Usage	2
Punctuation:	
Comma	3
Hyphen	3
Underlined Words	18
Spelling	5

THURSDAY   Week 13

<u>A Trip to the Moon</u> was the first science ~~fictian~~ fiction film
ever made and it was very successful One scene in particular
became famous. It shows a spaceship landing in the eye of
the proverbial "man in the moon." Even though many people
around the world saw the film Méliès did not ~~prophit~~ profit much
from its success Other people made ~~copys~~ copies of the film and
~~keeped~~ kept the profits for themselves

   Méliès is ~~remmembered~~ remembered today as one of the first to
use multiple exposures, time-lapse ~~fotografy~~ photography and hand-painted
color. Because of the sense of magic in his films Méliès is
sometimes called a "cinemagician".

Error Summary

Language Usage	1
Punctuation:	
Comma	4
Period	3
Quotation Mark	2
Underlined Words	5
Spelling	5

Name _____

WEDNESDAY   Week 13

Other filmmakers were making single shot films but Méliès linked nummerus shots together. In 1899, he released the seven minute film Cinderella which told the familiar ferry tale in 20 scenes. His best known film was relleased in 1902. Titled A Trip to the Moon it was loosely based on two books that were popular at the time. Those books were From the Earth to the Moon by Jules Verne and The First Men in the Moon by H. G. Wells. The film ran 14 minutes when perjected at 16 frames per second, the usual speed at the time. Today, movies are typical projected at 24 to 30 frames per second, so the motion is smoother and least chopy.

WATCH FOR
- commas
- hyphens
- movie titles
- book titles

THURSDAY   Week 13

A Trip to the Moon was the first science fictian film ever made and it was very successful One scene in particular became famous. It shows a spaceship landing in the eye of the proverbial "man in the moon. Even though many people around the world saw the film Méliès did not prophit much from its success Other people made copys of the film and keeped the profits for themselves

Méliès is remmembered today as one of the first to use multiple exposures, time-lapse fotografy and hand-painted color. Because of the sense of magic in his films Méliès is sometimes called a "cinemagician".

WATCH FOR
- commas
- special phrases in quotation marks
- punctuation with quotation marks

MONDAY   Week 14

Diary of a Science Genius

Monday January 15

    I've got to decide on a project for the science fair

this year, and fast! For my project last year, I made glue

from milk. The only ~~mattereals~~ [materials] I used were skim milk, vinegar,

water, and baking soda. I first heated the ~~vinagur~~ [vinegar] and milk.

The milk curdled, making something called "curds" and ~~leeving~~ [leaving]

a ~~likwid~~ [liquid] called "whey." Then I mixed the ~~dryed~~ [dried] curds with the

water and baking soda. The ~~mixchur~~ [mixture] formed glue. It really

worked! This year I want to do something even more exciting

~~then~~ [than] that, but I haven't thought of ~~nothing~~ [anything] yet.

Error Summary

Language Usage	2
Punctuation:	
Comma	6
Ellipses	1
Period	1
Quotation Mark	2
Spelling	6

TUESDAY   Week 14

tuesday, january 16

    I have a ~~grate~~ [great] idea for the science ~~fare~~ [fair]! Im going to

~~proov~~ [prove] that I can walk on top of a liquid with out sinking. I'll

need water, cornstarch, and some large plastic tubs. I think

I should use three tubs and line them up. Twelve boxes of

corn starch should be ~~enuff~~ [enough]. The first thing I'll do is put

cornstarch in the plastic tubs, then I'll pour in some water.

I'm ~~sposed~~ [supposed] to add the water a little at a time, then Ill mix

the stuff until its like thick pancake batter. If theres some

in each tub, I can walk from one to the other. I'll test it

out ~~tommorrow~~ [tomorrow]. I bet itll be messy!

Error Summary

Capitalization	4
Punctuation:	
Apostrophe	5
Comma	2
Exclamation Point	1
Period	2
Spelling	8

Name _____

MONDAY	Week 14

Diary of a Science Genius

Monday January 15

    I've got to decide on a project for the science fair this year..and fast! For my project last year I made glue from milk The only mattereals I used were skim milk vinegar water and baking soda. I first heated the vinagur and milk. The milk curdled, making something called "curds" and leeving a likwid called whey. Then I mixed the dryed curds with the water and baking soda. The mixchur formed glue. It really worked! This year I want to do something even more exciting then that but I haven't thought of nothing yet.

WATCH FOR
- commas
- ellipses
- special words in quotation marks

TUESDAY	Week 14

tuesday, january 16

    I have a grate idea for the science fare! Im going to proov that I can walk on top of a liquid with out sinking. I'll need water cornstarch and some large plastic tubs. I think I should use three tubs and line them up. Twelve boxes of corn starch should be enuff. The first thing I'll do is put cornstarch in the plastic tubs then I'll pour in some water. I'm sposed to add the water a little at a time, then Ill mix the stuff until its like thick pancake batter. If theres some in each tub, I can walk from one to the other. I'll test it out tommorow. I bet itll be messy

WATCH FOR
- commas
- apostrophes
- end punctuation

WEDNESDAY　　　　　　　　　　　　　　　Week 14

Wednesday
~~Wedensday~~, January 17

　　　　Well, I ~~tryed~~ (tried) the ~~ikspirimant~~ (experiment), it didnt work. Then I

reread the directions. The ~~misteak~~ (mistake) I made was not stomping

hard enough on the mixture. What I need to do is stomp

down very hard, this will make the goo ~~hardin~~ (harden) immediately.

That way, my feet wont sink. How does it work? Cornstarch,

unlike many other ~~substanses~~ (substances), does not ~~disolve~~ (dissolve) in water. A

hard ~~impack~~ (impact) causes more water to become ~~apsorbed~~ (absorbed) by

the microscopic grains of cornstarch. I have to be careful,

though. If the impact is too great, it will actually crack the

hard mixture. I'll try it again ~~tommorow~~ (tomorrow).

Error Summary

Capitalization	2
Punctuation:	
Apostrophe	2
Comma	3
Period	2
Question Mark	1
Spelling	10

THURSDAY　　　　　　　　　　　　　　　Week 14

Thursday, ~~Jannuary~~ (January) 18

　　　　The first thing I did after school today was, go to the

store, and buy more cornstarch. Yikes! This project is getting

~~expensif~~ (expensive). I was ~~determinned~~ (determined) to make the experiment work,

and I was ~~finnaly~~ (finally) successful. I mixed the cornstarch and

water in the three tubs again. Then, stomping hard enough

to ~~cawse~~ (cause) the mixture to harden for a ~~momment~~ (moment), I walked

from one tub to the other. Hooray! My feet didnt sink! This

experiment is so impressive that I'll probably win first prize

at the science fair. the next thing on my agenda: getting this

weeks math homework done.

Error Summary

Capitalization	1
Punctuation:	
Apostrophe	2
Comma	6
Exclamation Point	2
Spelling	6

Name _____

WEDNESDAY   Week 14

Wedensday, January 17

    Well I tryed the ikspirimant, it didnt work. Then I reread the directions. The misteak I made was not stomping hard enough on the mixture. What I need to do is stomp down very hard this will make the goo hardin immediately. That way, my feet wont sink. How does it work. Cornstarch unlike many other substanses does not disolve in water. A hard impack causes more water to become apsorbed by the microscopic grains of cornstarch. I have to be careful, though. If the impact is too great, it will actually crack the hard mixture. I'll try it again tommorow.

- commas
- run-on sentences
- apostrophes

THURSDAY   Week 14

Thursday Jannuary 18

    The first thing I did after school today was, go to the store, and buy more cornstarch. Yikes. This project is getting expensif. I was determinned to make the experiment work and I was finnaly successful. I mixed the cornstarch and water in the three tubs again. Then stomping hard enough to cawse the mixture to harden for a momment I walked from one tub to the other. Hooray. My feet didnt sink! This experiment is so impressive that I'll probably win first prize at the science fair. the next thing on my agenda: getting this weeks math homework done.

- commas
- end punctuation
- apostrophes

MONDAY   Week 15

Shipwreck!

The <u>Titanic</u> wasn't the only ~~luxery~~ *luxury* ship that sank in the atlantic ocean. In the summer of 1956, the <u>Andrea Doria</u> joined the <u>Titanic</u> on the ocean floor. Like the <u>Titanic</u>, the <u>Andrea Doria</u> was a grand ship. It was 212 meters (697 ft). long and could hold about 1,240 ~~pasengers~~ *passengers* and 560 crew members. It had three out_door ~~swiming~~ *swimming* pools, and many beautiful ~~valuble~~ *valuable* works of art. Most important, however, ~~was~~ *were* the many ~~safty~~ *safety* features that should ~~of~~ *have* kept the ship afloat. These features included radar, which was a relatively new invention in the 1950s. So, what caused the ship to sink?

Error Summary

Capitalization	2
Language Usage	2
Punctuation:	
Apostrophe	1
Comma	6
Period	1
Question Mark	1
Underlined Words	4
Spelling	6

TUESDAY   Week 15

On july 17, 1956, the <u>Andrea Doria</u> left genoa, Italy, and was headed for new york. The voyage was supposed to ~~took~~ *take* nine days. There were 1,706 people aboard, including passengers and crew. On July 25, just before 1100 P.M., the ship was south of nantucket island. It's radar detected another ship ~~approching~~ *approaching* from 17 nautical miles away. The ship was the <u>Stockholm</u>, a swedish passenger liner. The <u>Stockholm</u> also noticed the <u>Andrea Doria</u> on its radar. With so much ocean between them, it would seem that the crew could ~~of~~ *have* avoided an accident. Each ship made ~~adjustmunts~~ *adjustments* to widen the passing ~~distanse~~ *distance*, but each misjudged the other's course.

Error Summary

Capitalization	7
Language Usage	2
Punctuation:	
Apostrophe	2
Colon	1
Comma	3
Period	2
Underlined Words	5
Spelling	3

Name _____

MONDAY	Week 15

Shipwreck!

The <u>Titanic</u> wasnt the only luxery ship that sank in the atlantic ocean. In the summer of 1956 the <u>Andrea</u> <u>Doria</u> joined the Titanic on the ocean floor. Like the Titanic, the Andrea Doria was a grand ship. It was 212 meters (697 ft) long and could hold about 1,240 pasengers and 560 crew members. It had three out door swiming pools, and many beautiful valuble works of art. Most important however was the many safty features that should of kept the ship afloat. These features included radar which was a relatively new invention in the 1950s. So, what caused the ship to sink.

WATCH FOR
- names of ships
- place names
- abbreviations

TUESDAY	Week 15

On july 17 1956, the Andrea Doria left genoa Italy, and was headed for new york. The voyage was supposed to took nine days. There were 1,706 people aboard, including passengers and crew. On July 25, just before 1100 PM, the ship was south of nantucket island. It's radar detected another ship approching from 17 nautical miles away. The ship was the <u>Stockholm</u>, a swedish passenger liner. The Stockholm also noticed the Andrea Doria on its radar. With so much ocean between them, it would seem that the crew could of avoided an accident. Each ship made adjustmunts to widen the passing distanse but each misjudged the others course.

WATCH FOR
- dates
- names of ships
- place names
- time

WEDNESDAY   Week 15

The Andrea Doria was traveling in a ~~hevy~~ *heavy* fog that the Stockholm would soon encounter. ~~Niether~~ *Neither* could see the other and crew members made mistakes reading the radar. The swedish ship decided to pass on the port (left) side, and the italian ship chose to pass on the starboard (right) side. When they got within two nautical miles of each other it became clear that they were heading ~~direct~~ *directly* toward each other. At the speed they were traveling, it was ~~imposible~~ *impossible* for them to avoid a crash. At about 1110 PM, the Stockholm crashed into the starboard side of the Italian ship, cutting open seven of its ~~elevan~~ *eleven* decks. It was a fatal blow.

Error Summary

Capitalization	2
Language Usage	1
Punctuation:	
Colon	1
Comma	2
Parentheses	2
Period	2
Underlined Words	3
Spelling	4

THURSDAY   Week 15

The Stockholm was still sea worthy. This wasnt true of the Andrea Doria however. The loss of life ~~weren't~~ *wasn't* as bad as it coulda been. The ~~axident~~ *accident* left 51 people dead, most of them from the Andrea Doria. Nearby ships came to help, and the Stockholm provided extra life boats. By 530 the next morning, the last lifeboat ~~have~~ *had* left the andrea doria. At 1009 AM, she had ~~sank~~ *sunk* below the surface. The ship is now 76 meters (250 ft) below the ocean surface and is a popular deep-sea diving site. Its also a dangerous site, ~~oweing~~ *owing* to strong ~~curents~~ *currents* sharks and other ~~hazzerds~~ *hazards*. For this reason, it has often been ~~call~~ *called* the "mount everest" of scuba diving.

Error Summary

Capitalization	4
Language Usage	5
Punctuation:	
Apostrophe	2
Colon	2
Comma	3
Period	3
Underlined Words	6
Spelling	6

Name _____

WEDNESDAY	Week 15

The Andrea Doria was traveling in a hevy fog that the <u>Stockholm</u> would soon encounter. Niether could see the other and crew members made mistakes reading the radar. The swedish ship decided to pass on the port (left) side, and the italian ship chose to pass on the starboard right side. When they got within two nautical miles of each other it became clear that they were heading direct toward each other. At the speed they were traveling, it was imposible for them to avoid a crash. At about 1110 PM, the Stockholm crashed into the starboard side of the Italian ship, cutting open seven of its elevan decks. It was a fatal blow.

- nationalities
- time
- parentheses
- adverbs

THURSDAY	Week 15

The Stockholm was still sea worthy. This wasnt true of the Andrea Doria however. The loss of life weren't as bad as it coulda been. The axident left 51 people dead, most of them from the Andrea Doria. Nearby ships came to help, and the Stockholm provided extra life boats. By 530 the next morning, the last lifeboat have left the <u>andrea doria</u>. At 1009 AM, she had sank below the surface. The ship is now 76 meters (250 ft) below the ocean surface and is a popular deep-sea diving site. Its also a dangerous site, oweing to strong curents sharks and other hazzerds. For this reason, it has often been call the "mount everest" of scuba diving.

- verbs
- compound words
- place names

MONDAY

Week 16

The Amazing Spider

Have you ever wondered how a creature as small as
a ~~spidder~~ spider is able to weave a ~~intriccate~~ an intricate web? The ~~anser~~ answer

might be that spiders have huge brains! That's what some

scientists are ~~conclude~~ concluding. Biologists at universities in Costa

rica and Panama have studied tropical spiders of all sizes.

Their research has ~~shone~~ shown that smaller spiders have bigger

brains relative to ~~they're~~ their body size. In some species, the

~~sentrel~~ central nervous system which includes the ~~brane~~ brain fills nearly

80 percent of the spider's body. In some spiders, the central

nervous system even ~~spill~~ spills into their legs!

Error Summary

Capitalization	1
Language Usage	3
Punctuation:	
Apostrophe	2
Comma	2
Question Mark	1
Spelling	7

TUESDAY

Week 16

why ~~wood~~ would scientists study spider brains? Well, scientists
are ~~curius~~ curious people in general these biologists were mostly
~~wandering~~ wondering how spider's formed webs. In their study, they

first ~~compaired~~ compared the webs spun by big spiders with those

spun by little spiders. They noticed that the one's spun by

puny spiders were just as intricate as those spun by giant

spiders. They ~~speckuladed~~ speculated that web-spinning, which ~~apears~~ appears to

be a complex behavior, requires considerable brain activity.

The results of the scientists study seem to ~~confurm~~ confirm this the
fact that small spiders brain's are bigger in ~~perpershun~~ proportion to

their body sizes ~~sugests~~ suggests that web-spinning takes brain power.

Error Summary

Capitalization	3
Punctuation:	
Apostrophe	5
Period	2
Spelling	9

Name _____

The Amazing Spider

Have you ever wondered how a creature as small as a spidder is able to weave a intriccate web. The anser might be that spiders have huge brains! Thats what some scientists are conclude. Biologists at universities in Costa rica and Panama have studied tropical spiders of all sizes. Their research has shone that smaller spiders have bigger brains relative to they're body size. In some species, the sentrel nervous system which includes the brane fills nearly 80 percent of the spiders body. In some spiders, the central nervous system even spill into their legs!

- articles
- apostrophes
- verbs

why wood scientists study spider brains? Well, scientists are curius people in general, these biologists were mostly wandering how spider's formed webs. In their study, they first compaired the webs spun by big spiders with those spun by little spiders. They noticed that the one's spun by puny spiders were just as intricate as those spun by giant spiders. They speckuladed that web-spinning, which apears to be a complex behavior, requires considerable brain activity. The results of the scientists study seem to confurm this, the fact that small spiders brain's are bigger in perporshun to their body sizes sugests that web-spinning takes brain power.

- apostrophes
- run-on sentences

WEDNESDAY　　　　　　　　　　　Week 16

　　　　　are
　　Spiders ~~is~~ also amazing because of their legs. One

difference
~~difference~~ between spiders and insects ~~are~~ that spiders
　　　　　　　　　　　　　　　　　　　　is

　　　　　　　　　　　　　　than
have eight legs rather ~~then~~ six legs. However, a group of

　　　　　　　　　　　　　　　　　recently
researchers in France concluded ~~rescently~~ that spiders may

have more legs than they really need. These scientists

collected
~~colected~~ thousands of spiders in the wild, and they noticed

　　　　　　　　　　　　　　　　　　　least
that more than 10 percent had lost at ~~lest~~ one leg. They

wondered if the missing legs were a disadvantage, so they

　　　　　　　　an
conducted ~~a~~ experiment. They placed 60 intact spiders in

separate
~~seperate~~ boxes and placed 63 spiders missing one or more

legs in another set of boxes. the results were surprising.

THURSDAY　　　　　　　　　　　Week 16

　　The spiders missing one leg made webs that were not

　　　　　different　　　　　　　　　built
much ~~diferent~~ from the webs ~~bilt~~ by intact spiders. The

　　　　　　　　　　　　　　　　　　　Moreover
same was true of spiders missing two legs. ~~Morever~~, all of

　　　　　were
the spiders ~~was~~ equally able to catch and eat insects. This

　　　　led
finding ~~lead~~ the scientists to conclude that spiders have more

legs than they need. However, the scientists also found that

there　　　　limit
~~their~~ was a ~~limmit~~ to the number of legs a spider could

lose
~~loose~~. The team found very few five-legged spiders in the

wild. This suggests that spiders cannot survive ~~easy~~ if they
　　　　　　　　　　　　　　　　　　　　　　　　easily

　　　　　　　　　　　　　laboratory
lose too many legs. In the ~~labratory~~, spiders with five legs

　　　　　　　　　　　　　　　　　　　　　　　faulty
were able to build webs, but the webs were ~~fawlty~~.

Name _____

WEDNESDAY   Week 16

Spiders is also amazing because of their legs. One differance between spiders and insects are that spiders have eight legs rather then six legs. However a group of researchers in France concluded rescently that spiders may have more legs than they really need. These scientists colected thousands of spiders in the wild and they noticed that more than 10 percent had lost at lest one leg. They wondered if the missing legs were a disadvantage so they conducted a experiment. They placed 60 intact spiders in seperate boxes and placed 63 spiders missing one or more legs in another set of boxes, the results were surprising.

- commas
- verbs
- run-on sentences

THURSDAY   Week 16

The spiders missing one leg made webs that were not much diferent from the webs bilt by intact spiders. The same was true of spiders missing two legs. Morover, all of the spiders was equally able to catch and eat insects. This finding lead the scientists to conclude that spiders have more legs than they need. However the scientists also found that their was a limmit to the number of legs a spider could loose. The team found very few five legged spiders in the wild. This suggests that spiders cannot survive easy if they lose too many legs. In the labratory, spiders with five legs were able to build webs, but the webs were fawlty.

- verbs
- hyphens

MONDAY
Week 17

The French Spider-Man

Alain Robert (roh-BAYR) was born on august 7 1962 in a small town in Bourgogne France. Famous for climbing skyscrapers, he is known as the "french Spider-Man", named
hero
for the comic book heroe. As a boy, Robert used to scale
cliffs
the rock clifs near his home. Thats how his interest in climbing began. He scaled his first building when he was just
forgotten
12 years old. On that day, he had forgoten his keys and was
apartment
locked out of his parents appartment on the eighth floor.
decided
Instead of waiting for his folk's to get home he desided to
building
climb the outside wall of the bilding and let himself in.

Error Summary

Capitalization	2
Punctuation:	
Apostrophe	3
Comma	4
Quotation Mark	1
Spelling	6

TUESDAY
Week 17

"Climbing is my passion, my philosophy of life, Robert says. Robert's passion became apparent in 1982. He had two accidents that year. The first one was in january, the second one was in september. Both times he fell 15 meters
fracturing
(49 ft) and was badly hurt. Besides frackshuring bones,
suffered
he also sufferred brain injuries that resulted in vertigo a
Doctors
condition that causes him to feel dizzy. Docters declared him disabled and told him to give up his passion but he was climbing again within six months. Since then, he has climbed
structures
increasingly more challenging struktures, including more than 70 skyscrapers around the world.

Error Summary

Capitalization	2
Punctuation:	
Comma	2
Parentheses	1
Period	1
Quotation Mark	2
Semicolon	1
Spelling	4

Name _____

The French Spider-Man

Alain Robert (roh-BAYR) was born on august 7 1962 in a small town in Bourgogne France. Famous for climbing skyscrapers, he is known as the "french Spider-Man", named for the comic book heroe. As a boy, Robert used to scale the rock clifs near his home. Thats how his interest in climbing began. He scaled his first building when he was just 12 years old. On that day, he had forgotten his keys and was locked out of his parents appartment on the eighth floor. Instead of waiting for his folk's to get home he desided to climb the outside wall of the bilding and let himself in.

WATCH FOR

• dates
• nationalities
• punctuation with quotation marks
• apostrophes

Climbing is my passion, my philosophy of life, Robert says. Robert's passion became apparent in 1982. He had two accidents that year. The first one was in january the second one was in september. Both times he fell 15 meters (49 ft and was badly hurt. Besides frackshuring bones, he also suffered brain injuries that resulted in vertigo a condition that causes him to feel dizzy. Docters declared him disabled and told him to give up his passion but he was climbing again within six months. Since then, he has climbed increasingly more challenging struktures, including more than 70 skyscrapers around the world.

WATCH FOR

• quotation marks
• semicolons
• abbreviations
• parentheses

WEDNESDAY   Week 17

skyscrapers
People need permits to climb ~~skyscrappers~~. It's

permission
such a dangerous activity that ~~permision~~ is often denied.

strategy   is
Robert's ~~strattegy~~ ~~are~~ simply to arrive at dawn, ready to

climb, before anyone can stop him. As he climbs crowds of

illegal
onlookers gather. The activity is ~~illeagle~~, and Robert has been

arrested   enforcement officials
~~arrested~~ many times. Law ~~inforcemunt~~ ~~offishals~~ often wait for

him to finish climbing sometimes they stop him earlier. That's

what happened in 1997 at the petronas Twin Towers in Kuala

Lumpur, malaysia. At the time the towers were the worlds

tallest
~~most tall~~ buildings. Malaysian authorities arrested Robert on

the 60th floor, 28 floors from the top.

Error Summary

Capitalization	2
Language Usage	2
Punctuation:	
Apostrophe	4
Comma	2
Semicolon	1
Spelling	7

THURSDAY   Week 17

In 1999, Robert faced the most dangerous climbing

conditions   career
~~conditons~~ of his ~~carreer~~. He was on the 108-story Sears

Tower now called willis tower in Chicago. When he was 20

floors from the top a thick fog rolled in and covered the

glass-and-metal wall with moisture It was so slippery that

fortunately
Robert was in serious danger. ~~fortunately~~, he was able to

difficulties
overcome these ~~dificculties~~ and reach the top. This dangerous

incident
~~insident~~ did not stop him, though. Robert continues with his

adventures as an extreme climber. Because he usually uses

amaze
only his bare hands and special shoes his exploits ~~ammaze~~

every one who watches him.

Error Summary

Capitalization	3
Punctuation:	
Comma	5
Period	1
Hyphen	1
Spelling	6

Name _____

WEDNESDAY   Week 17

People need permits to climb skyscrappers. Its such a dangerous activity that permision is often denied. Roberts strattegy are simply to arrive at dawn, ready to climb, before anyone can stop him. As he climbs crowds of onlookers gather. The activity is illeagle, and Robert has been arested many times. Law inforcemunt offishals often wait for him to finish climbing, sometimes they stop him earlier. Thats what happened in 1997 at the petronas Twin Towers in Kuala Lumpur, malaysia. At the time the towers were the worlds most tall buildings. Malaysian authorities arrested Robert on the 60th floor, 28 floors from the top.

- commas
- apostrophes
- names of buildings
- semicolons

THURSDAY   Week 17

In 1999, Robert faced the most dangerous climbing conditons of his carreer. He was on the 108 story Sears Tower now called willis tower in Chicago. When he was 20 floors from the top a thick fog rolled in, and covered the glass-and-metal wall with moisture It was so slippery that Robert was in serious danger. fortunately, he was able to overcome these difcculties and reach the top. This dangerous insident did not stop him, though. Robert continues with his adventures as an extreme climber. Because he usually uses only his bare hands and special shoes his exploits ammaze every one who watches him.

- hyphens
- names of buildings
- commas

MONDAY   Week 18

Champions of Equality

The right to vote is ~~an~~ a fundamental right that many

people take for ~~granite~~ granted. these people have forgotten—or

never knew about—the struggle in this Country to secure

~~voteing~~ voting rights for all. One of the leaders in the fight for

women's ~~Right~~ right to ~~Vote~~ vote was Susan B. Anthony. She was one of

the first ~~americans~~ americans to stand up for women's rights. Born into

a ~~quaker~~ quaker family in 1820, ~~her family taught her~~ she learned that the law

should ~~guarentee~~ guarantee equal rights for all men and women. After

she became a schoolteacher at age ~~ninteen~~ nineteen, she taught her

students these same ~~valyooz~~ values.

Error Summary

Capitalization	6
Language Usage	1
Punctuation:	
Comma	1
Period	2
Sentence Structure	1
Spelling	5

TUESDAY   Week 18

Eventually, however, she wanted a ~~more large~~ larger ~~audiense~~ audience.

She ~~tryed~~ tried to speak at political rallies, but she soon found out

that only men ~~was~~ were permitted to address the crowds. In 1851,

she met ~~elizabeth cady stanton~~ elizabeth cady stanton, another ~~champeun~~ champion of women's

rights. They soon became close ~~freinds~~ friends and started working

together toward the same ~~goles~~ goals. Stanton had ~~all ready~~ already ~~wrote~~ written

an important document promoting the cause of ~~ekwality~~ equality. She

based her document on the ~~declaration of independence~~ declaration of independence,

changing one line to read, "All men and women are created

equal". When the ~~civil war~~ civil war began in 1861, both ~~woman~~ women joined

in the fight against slavery.

Error Summary

Capitalization	7
Language Usage	4
Punctuation:	
Comma	4
Quotation Mark	1
Spelling	7

Name _____

MONDAY   Week 18

Champions of Equality

The right to vote is an fundamental right that many people take for granite, these people have forgotten—or never knew about—the struggle in this Country to secure voteing rights for all. One of the leaders in the fight for women's Right to Vote was Susan B Anthony. She was one of the first americans to stand up for women's rights. Born into a quaker family in 1820, her family taught her that the law should guarentee equal rights for all men and women. After she became a schoolteacher at age ninteen she taught her students these same valyooz.

- abbreviations
- nationalities
- names of religious groups
- dangling modifiers

TUESDAY   Week 18

Eventually however she wanted a more large audiense. She tryed to speak at political rallies but she soon found out that only men was permitted to address the crowds. In 1851, she met elizabeth cady stanton, another champeun of women's rights. They soon became close freinds and started working together toward the same goles. Stanton had all ready wrote an important document promoting the cause of ekwality. She based her document on the declaration of independence, changing one line to read, "All men and women are created equal". When the civil war began in 1861 both woman joined in the fight against slavery.

- words that compare
- historical documents
- historic events
- punctuation with quotation marks

WEDNESDAY   Week 18

Both women knew the words of "The Star-Spangled
Banner," a ~~poppular~~ popular song at the time. Anthony was ~~trubbled~~ troubled by
one phrase in the song: "the land of the free". for a country
that allowed slavery, these words seemed like a ~~lye~~ lie. Anthony
and Stanton both supported the antislavery movement. when
the war ended in 1865, though they broke away from it. They
were ~~disapointed~~ disappointed because other members of the movement
showed little ~~interust~~ interest in womens' right to vote. Those people
supported the Fifteenth Amendment to the constitution which
secured voting rights for African American men. Women,
however, were still denied the ~~write~~ right to vote.

Error Summary

Capitalization	3
Punctuation:	
Apostrophe	1
Comma	7
Quotation Mark	3
Spelling	6

THURSDAY   Week 18

anthony and stanton began working toward ~~a~~ an amendment
that would grant voting rights to ~~woman~~ women. From 1868 to 1870,
Anthony ~~pubblished~~ published a ~~weakly~~ weekly ~~maggazeen~~ magazine supporting the cause.
In 1872, Anthony ~~done~~ did something that brought her national
attention: She voted in the Presidential election in Rochester,
new york. Since this was against the law, she was arrested
and brought to ~~trail~~ trial. In an ~~emotionel~~ emotional speech, she defended
herself. She said that acting against an unfair law ~~were~~ was
brave and ~~admireable~~ admirable. Sadly, Anthony did not see the results
of her work. She died in 1906, fourteen years before the
~~Ninteenth~~ Nineteenth Amendment ~~were~~ was passed.

Error Summary

Capitalization	5
Language Usage	5
Punctuation:	
Comma	1
Spelling	7

Name _____

| WEDNESDAY | Week 18 |

Both women knew the words of The Star-Spangled Banner a poppular song at the time. Anthony was trubbled by one phrase in the song: "the land of the free". for a country that allowed slavery these words seemed like a lye. Anthony and Stanton both supported the antislavery movement. when the war ended in 1865 though they broke away from it. They were disapointed because other members of the movement showed little interust in womens' right to vote. Those people supported the Fifteenth Amendment to the constitution which secured voting rights for African American men. Women however were still denied the write to vote.

- song titles
- historical documents
- punctuation with quotation marks

| THURSDAY | Week 18 |

anthony and stanton began working toward a amendment that would grant voting rights to woman. From 1868 to 1870, Anthony pubblished a weakly maggazeen supporting the cause. In 1872, Anthony done something that brought her national attention: She voted in the Presidential election in Rochester, new york. Since this was against the law she was arrested and brought to trail. In an emotionol speech, she defended herself. She said that acting against an unfair law were brave and admireable. Sadly, Anthony did not see the results of her work. She died in 1906, fourteen years before the Ninteenth Amendment were passed.

- place names
- verbs

MONDAY   Week 19

Four Days Without a Cellphone

I arrived at school on monday morning, and reach into my pocket for my cellphone. I wanted to text a friend but couldn't locate my phone. I didn't panic at first. I reached into another pocket, then my back pack, and than my locker. Then I panicked I had lost my preshuss phone and felt throughly cut off from the world (although there were people all around me. How could I function without my phone: I used it for everything: innertanement, connecting with freinds, and getting school assinements. My phone was practically an extension of my brain how did this happen?

Corrections marked: reached · monday (cap) · couldn't · didn't · then · precious · thoroughly · world, · me.? · phone. · entertainment · friends · assignments

Error Summary

Capitalization	2
Language Usage	2
Punctuation:	
Apostrophe	2
Comma	2
Parentheses	1
Period	2
Question Mark	2
Spelling	6

Handwritten note: I think need period after Parenthesis. Yes!

TUESDAY   Week 19

By Wenesday, the loss of my phone had made my life chalenging. First, I forgot my p.e. clothes because I didn't gets the voice memo that always reminded me to bring them to school each weak. I couldn't text mom to bring them so I had to wait to use the school office phone after class. Than I was late to PE. class. Worse of all, my friends went out for ice cream after school. They had invited me but it was two late when I found out because I didn't get the message. I wondered why my friend's made plans only through text messaging and not in person? Its probably because my friends and me are use to texting each other.

Corrections marked: Wednesday · challenging · clothes. · get · voice · week · mom (cap) · them. · Then · Worst · too · because. · friends · person. It's · I · used

Error Summary

Capitalization	5
Language Usage	5
Punctuation:	
Apostrophe	3
Comma	4
Period	3
Spelling	4

Name _____

Four Days Without a Cellphone

I arrived at school on monday morning, and reach into my pocket for my cellphone. I wanted to text a friend but couldnt locate my phone. I didnt panic at first. I reached into another pocket, then my back pack, and than my locker. Then I panicked I had lost my preshuss phone and felt throughly cut off from the world, (although there were people all around me.) How could I function without my phone! I used it for everything: innertanement, connecting with freinds, and getting school assinements. My phone was practically an extension of my brain how did this happen.

• parentheses
• run-on sentences
• end punctuation

By Wenesday, the loss of my phone had made my life chalenging. First, I forgot my p.e. clothes. Because I didn't gets the Voice memo that always reminded me to bring them to school each weak. I couldnt text mom to bring them so I had to wait to use the school office phone after class. Than I was late to PE. class. Worse of all, my friends went out for ice cream after school. They had invited me but it was two late when I found out because, I didn't get the message. I wondered why my friend's made plans only through text messaging, and not in person? Its probably because my friends and me are use to texting each other.

• abbreviations
• incomplete sentences
• pronouns
• words that compare

WEDNESDAY   Week 19

My Mom kept saying that my phone would turn up, but I knew that I needed to ~~found~~ find a solution mean while. So on thursday, I distributed my home phone number to my friends. Some of them ~~groan~~ groaned about the inconvenience of having to call rather ~~then~~ than text, but I pointed out that it was my only option. Anyway, part of me genuinely thought it ~~would'nt~~ wouldn't be so bad, to have real ~~convirsashuns~~ conversations with them for a change. That night, I waited by the home phone for hours, But it didn't ~~never~~ even ring once. I was so bored. Usually when I'm stuck some where and need to pass the time, I play games on my cellphone. Mom told me to clean my room. Yeah, right.

Error Summary

Capitalization	3
Language Usage	4
Punctuation:	
Apostrophe	2
Comma	6
Period	1
Spelling	4

THURSDAY   Week 19

When I left the room ~~brief~~ briefly, I thought I heard ~~a~~ an ~~unfimiliar~~ unfamiliar sound, like the ringing of ~~a~~ an alarm clock. My mom called to me from the other room and told me that "a friend had called." When I ~~inkwired~~ inquired further, she said she didn't get a name, or a phone number. I realized that even if she had ~~got~~ gotten the name, I didn't have ~~no~~ any numbers ~~memerized~~ memorized; ~~their~~ they're all programmed into my phone. ~~Disipointid~~ Disappointed, I ran up to my bedroom (which was still messy), closed the door, ~~streched~~ stretched out on my bed, and stared at the floor. Lying there, I ~~sudden~~ suddenly noticed my phone sticking out from under the bed. Yay! Now, where did I ~~left~~ leave my phone charger?

Error Summary

Language Usage	7
Punctuation:	
Comma	3
Exclamation Point	1
Hyphen	1
Question Mark	1
Quotation Mark	2
Spelling	6

Name _____

| **WEDNESDAY** | **Week 19** |

- commas
- double negatives
- compound words

    My Mom kept saying that my phone would turn up but I knew that I needed to found a solution mean while. So on thursday, I distributed my home phone number to my friends. Some of them groan about the inconvenience of having to call rather then text but I pointed out that it was my only option. Anyway part of me genuinely thought it would'nt be so bad, to have real convirsashuns with them for a change. That night, I waited by the home phone for hours. But it didnt never even ring once. I was so bored Usually when Im stuck some where and need to pass the time, I play games on my cellphone. Mom told me to clean my room. Yeah right.

| **THURSDAY** | **Week 19** |

- adverbs
- hyphens
- end punctuation

    When I left the room brief, I thought I heard a unfimiliar sound, like the ringing of a alarm clock. My mom called to me from the other room and told me that "a friend had called." When I inkwired further she said she didn't get a name, or a phone number. I realized that even if she had got the name, I didn't have no numbers memerized; their all programmed into my phone. Disipointid, I ran up to my bedroom (which was still messy) closed the door, streched out on my bed, and stared at the floor. Lying there, I sudden noticed my phone sticking-out from under the bed. Yay. Now, where did I left my phone charger.

MONDAY   Week 20

Pink Flamingos

These wading birds have a distinctive ~~apearince~~ appearance, with plumage in various shades of pink and orange. As much as 5 feet (1.52 meters) tall a flamingo is ~~empressive~~ impressive. It has a long, flexible neck and a thick bill that curves down ward. There ~~is~~ are five species of flamingos but all of them ~~has certin~~ have certain things in common, including slender legs and webbed feet.

Highly sociable birds, flamingos gather in huge ~~flox~~ flocks. If you see a group in ~~flite~~ flight you won't ~~never~~ ever forget the breathtaking sight. Hundreds of the birds fly in formation, with their outstretched necks and their broad wings ~~flaping~~ flapping.

Error Summary

Capitalization	1
Language Usage	3
Punctuation:	
Apostrophe	1
Comma	4
Parentheses	1
Spelling	7

TUESDAY   Week 20

When at rest flamingos present ~~a~~ an equally ~~intirsting~~ interesting sight. Their supple necks twist, and coil with ease over their bodies. ~~Flammingos~~ Flamingos are also famous for their one-legged poses. While wading in shallow water, they stand on one leg and tuck the other leg up into the body. Did you ever wonder why they ~~does~~ do this? Scientists ~~has~~ have offered various reasons for this ~~behavyur~~ behavior. One ~~posible~~ possible reason, is that it helps the birds conserve energy and ~~reggulate~~ regulate their body temperature. Another possible reason is that it ~~reduce~~ reduces ~~fahteeg~~ fatigue. Yet another possibility is that the flamingos simply want to dry out ~~its~~ their legs.

Error Summary

Language Usage	5
Punctuation:	
Comma	3
Hyphen	1
Question Mark	1
Spelling	6

Name _____

Pink Flamingos

These wading birds have a distinctive apearince, with plumage in various shades of pink and orange. As much as 5 feet 1.52 meters) tall a Flamingo is empressive. It has a long flexible neck and a thick bill that curves down ward. There is five species of flamingos but all of them has certin things in common, including slender legs and webbed feet.

Highly sociable birds, flamingos gather in huge flox. If you see a group in flite you wont never forget the breathtaking sight. Hundreds of the birds fly in formation, with their outstretched necks and their broad wings flaping.

- commas
- parentheses
- double negatives

When at rest flamingos present a equally intirsting sight. Their supple necks twist, and coil with ease over their bodies. Flammingos are also famous for their one legged poses. While wading in shallow water, they stand on one leg and tuck the other leg up into the body. Did you ever wonder why they does this. Scientists has offered various reasons for this behavyur. One posible reason, is that it helps the birds conserve energy and reggulate their body temperature. Another possible reason is that it reduce fahteeg. Yet another possibility is that the flamingos simply want to dry out its legs.

- hyphens
- end punctuation
- verbs
- possessives

WEDNESDAY　　　　　　　　　　　　　　Week 20

　　　　　　　　　　　　　　characteristic　　　　　　　　is
　　Another interesting ~~characteristick~~ of flamingos ~~are~~
　　　　　　　　　　　　　　　　shallow
the way they eat. Standing in ~~shalow~~ water, the birds stomp
their　　　　　　　　　agitate
~~there~~ webbed feet to ~~aggitate~~ the mud. A flamingo hold's its

curved bill underwater and swings its head from side to side,

swishing muddy water into its bill with its thick tongue. Tiny
　　　　　　　　　　　　　　　　　act
comb-like structures in the bill ~~acts~~ as filters. They strain
　　　　　　　　　　　　　　edible
algae, tiny mollusks, and other ~~eddibul~~ organisms from the

water in the same way that a colander strains pasta. The
　　　　　　　　　　　　　　　　　　　unique
filter-feeding system in the flamingos bill is ~~unnique~~. No other

birds have this feature. It's the birds food supply that gives

the flamingo it's pinkish or reddish color.

Error Summary

Language Usage	2
Punctuation:	
Apostrophe	5
Comma	2
Hyphen	2
Spelling	6

THURSDAY　　　　　　　　　　　　　　Week 20

　　When it is time to breed, flamingos gather in huge

groups on the lake shore. In fact, more than a million
　　　　gather　　　　　　　　　　　　　　　　　　breed
birds ~~gathers~~ on some large lakes in East africa to ~~brede~~.

Flamingos make nest's of muddy clay piled several inches high

into a cone shape. The female typically lays a single egg at
　　　　　　　　　　take
a time. Both parents ~~takes~~ care of the egg during the month

before hatching. Chicks are snowy-white or gray at first. Two

or three days after hatching, the young can leave the nest.
　　　　　　　　　　　　　　　partially
Adults feed the off spring ~~parshally~~ digested food that they
　　　　　　takes
regurgitate. It ~~take~~ time, though, for the babies to turn
　　　then　　　　　　　　　　　　　　　　were
pink. Until ~~than~~ you might not even know they ~~was~~ flamingos!

Error Summary

Capitalization	1
Language Usage	5
Punctuation:	
Apostrophe	1
Comma	4
Spelling	4

Name _____

WEDNESDAY　　　　　　　　　　　　Week 20

Another interesting characteristick of flamingos are the way they eat. Standing in shalow water, the birds stomp there webbed feet to aggitate the mud. A flamingo hold's its curved bill underwater and swings its head from side to side, swishing muddy water into its bill with its thick tongue. Tiny comb like structures in the bill acts as filters. They strain algae tiny mollusks and other eddibul organisms from the water in the same way that a colander strains pasta. The filter feeding system in the flamingos bill is unnique. No other birds have this feature. Its the birds food supply that gives the flamingo it's pinkish or reddish color.

- apostrophes
- verbs
- hyphens

THURSDAY　　　　　　　　　　　　Week 20

When it is time to breed flamingos gather in huge groups on the lake shore. In fact more than a million birds gathers on some large lakes in East africa to brede. Flamingos make nest's of muddy clay piled several inches high into a cone shape. The female typically lays a single egg at a time. Both parents takes care of the egg during the month before hatching. Chicks are snowy-white or gray at first. Two or three days after hatching the young can leave the nest. Adults feed the off spring parshally digested food that they regurgitate. It take time, though, for the babies to turn pink. Until than you might not even know they was flamingos!

- commas
- place names
- compound words

MONDAY	Week 21

Error Summary

Capitalization	11
Punctuation:	
Apostrophe	2
Comma	4
Exclamation Point	1
Period	3
Spelling	4

Four Letters

Dear aunt Pat

    Thank you so much for the awsome [awesome] birthday gift your generous gennerous [generous] check will be put to good use this summer. mom and dad are takeing [taking] me to egypt for the vacation of a lifetime I am so excited! We've been studying Egypt in my History class and Im looking forward to seeing the peeramids [pyramids] at giza. After that we'll visit the valley of the kings. I'll bring back a nice souvenir for you

        Your loving Nephew

        Kurt

TUESDAY	Week 21

Error Summary

Capitalization	5
Punctuation:	
Apostrophe	3
Comma	2
Exclamation Point	1
Question Mark	1
Spelling	3

Dear Kurt

    It was grate [great] to hear from you. Your vacation plans sound amazing! Dont forget to take lot's of pictures.

    You may not be aware that I studied archaeology in college. I did fieldwork in Egypt and even examined some of the artifax [artifacts] found in Tutankhamens tomb. Since then Archaeologists have learned much more about king tut and have even determend [determined] why he died at such a young age. Would you like to know what they have discovered?

        Love,

        aunt pat

Name _____

Four Letters

Dear aunt Pat

    Thank you so much for the awsome birthday gift, your gennerous check will be put to good use this Summer. mom and dad are takeing me to egypt for the vacation of a lifetime, I am so excited Weve been studying Egypt in my History class and Im looking forward to seeing the peeramids at giza. After that we'll visit the valley of the kings. I'll bring back a nice souvenir for you

        Your loving Nephew

        Kurt

- personal names
- place names
- run-on sentences
- end punctuation

Dear Kurt

    It was grate to hear from you. Your vacation plans sound amazing Dont forget to take lot's of pictures.

    You may not be aware that I studied archaeology in college. I did fieldwork in Egypt and even examined some of the artifax found in Tutankhamens tomb. Since then Archaeologists have learned much more about king tut and have even determend why he died at such a young age. Would you like to know what they have discovered.

        Love,

        aunt pat

- apostrophes
- end punctuation

WEDNESDAY　　　　　　　　　　　　　Week 21

Dear Aunt pat

　　　You bet Id like to know! All I know about King Tut so far is that he became king after his father's death. Tut was only about nine years old at the time. He died about ten years later but I don't think archaeologists knows why. Tut's toom is the only one in the Valley of the Kings that wasnt robbed by ancient tomb raders. when we go to the egyptian Museum in cairo we'll see the trezures that was found when Tuts tomb was excavated in 1922. What else do you know

（know, tomb, raiders, treasures, were annotations)

　　　　　　Your curious nephew

　　　　　　　kurt

Error Summary

Capitalization	5
Language Usage	2
Punctuation:	
Apostrophe	4
Comma	4
Question Mark	1
Spelling	3

THURSDAY　　　　　　　　　　　　　Week 21

Dear Kurt

　　　Did you know that more than 100 walking canes were found in Tut's tomb Scientists wondered why. X-rays and an CT scan of the mummy riveeled that Tut had sufferred from a bone disease. Because his bones broke easily he used a cane to keep from falling. Other tests showed that he also had Malaria. Most likely, the young king died from a combanation of a broken leg, a infekshun and malaria.

（a, revealed, suffered, combination, an infection annotations)

　　　Enjoy your trip, and Ill see you when you get back

　　　　　　Love,

　　　　　　Aunt pat

Error Summary

Capitalization	2
Language Usage	2
Punctuation:	
Apostrophe	1
Comma	3
Period	1
Question Mark	1
Spelling	4

Name _____

WEDNESDAY　　　　　　　　　　Week 21

Dear Aunt pat

　　You bet Id like to know! All I know about King Tut so far is that he became king after his fathers death. Tut was only about nine years old at the time. He died about ten years later but I don't think archaeologists knows why. Tut's toom is the only one in the Valley of the Kings that wasnt robbed by ancient tomb raders. when we go to the egyptian Museum in cairo we'll see the trezures that was found when Tuts tomb was excavated in 1922. What else do you know

　　　　　　Your curious nephew

　　　　　　kurt

- nationalities
- place names
- personal names
- apostrophes

THURSDAY　　　　　　　　　　Week 21

Dear Kurt

　　Did you know that more than 100 walking canes were found in Tut's tomb. Scientists wondered why. X-rays and an CT scan of the mummy riveeled that Tut had sufferred from a bone disease. Because his bones broke easily he used a cane to keep from falling. Other tests showed that he also had Malaria. Most likely, the young king died from a combanation of a broken leg, a infekshun and malaria.

　　　　Enjoy your trip, and Ill see you when you get back

　　　　　　Love,

　　　　　　Aunt pat

- end punctuation
- commas

MONDAY   Week 22

Error Summary

Capitalization	4
Language Usage	2
Punctuation:	
Comma	3
Quotation Mark	2
Spelling	4

Harbor Porpoises Make Comeback

January 2012. After a 65-year ~~abscence~~ [absence], harbor porpoises ~~begun~~ [began] returning to the San Francisco bay last month. They had last been seen in the area shortly before world war II. Wartime activities and poor water ~~quallity~~ [quality] ~~drived~~ [drove] away the small timid porpoises. Shipbuilding, an important ~~indistree~~ [industry] in the area at the time, contributed to the bay's polluted waters. Naomi Beeck a ~~resercher~~ [researcher] who studies the porpoises remembers, "My family lived in the nearby city of oakland in the 1940s. My mom recalls how awful the bay was then. The stench was dreadful."

TUESDAY   Week 22

Error Summary

Capitalization	4
Punctuation:	
Apostrophe	3
Comma	3
Question Mark	1
Spelling	7

The 1972 ~~passige~~ [passage] of the clean water Act ~~lead~~ [led] to an improvement in the water quality of the bay. So, why didn't the porpoises return in the 1970s? The reason is that the porpoises' food supply hadn't returned yet. It took time for the bay to ~~reccover~~ [recover] from the pollution and for the schools of Herring and Anchovies to return. Now, at last, conditions in the bay have improved ~~suffishuntly~~ [sufficiently] to support marine life. Meanwhile, many ~~gennerations~~ [generations] of harbor porpoises have been born over this 65-year period. Consequently, the bay was no ~~dout~~ [doubt] erased from the animals' memories. Perhaps harbor porpoises simply rediscovered the bay by ~~acsident~~ [accident].

Name _____

MONDAY   Week 22

• place names
• historic events
• verbs
• quotation marks

Harbor Porpoises Make Comeback

January 2012. After a 65-year abscence, harbor porpoises begun returning to the San Francisco bay last month. They had last been seen in the area shortly before world war II. Wartime activities and poor water quallity drived away the small timid porpoises. Shipbuilding, an important indistree in the area at the time, contributed to the bay's polluted waters. Naomi Beeck a resercher who studies the porpoises remembers, My family lived in the nearby city of oakland in the 1940s. My mom recalls how awful the bay was then. The stench was dreadful.

TUESDAY   Week 22

• names of laws
• apostrophes
• commas

The 1972 passige of the clean water Act lead to an improvement in the water quality of the bay. So, why didnt the porpoises return in the 1970s The reason is that the porpoises' food supply hadnt returned yet. It took time for the bay to reccover from the pollution and for the schools of Herring and Anchovies to return. Now at last conditions in the bay have improved suffishuntly to support marine life. Meanwhile, many gennerations of harbor porpoises have been born over this 65-year period. Consequently the bay was no dout erased from the animals memories. Perhaps harbor porpoises simply rediscovered the bay by acsident.

WEDNESDAY　　　Week 22

What else besides water quality may have ~~drove~~ driven away the harbor porpoises? Many things ~~was~~ were going on during the 1940s that might have frightened the shy animals. For one thing, the San Francisco Bay certainly was a ~~busseling~~ bustling place. The US Navy put ~~a~~ an underwater net across the ~~entrunse~~ entrance to the bay. This net which was seven miles long was installed to prevent enemy ~~submireens~~ submarines from entering the bay. In addition the ~~millitery~~ military set hundreds of mines just outside the Golden Gate. All of this activity plus the water pollution caused by manufacturing and raw sewage made the bay ~~a~~ an ~~unfaverible~~ unfavorable place for porpoises to live.

Error Summary

Language Usage	4
Punctuation:	
Comma	5
Period	2
Question Mark	1
Spelling	5

THURSDAY　　　Week 22

Harbor porpoises are smaller ~~then~~ than most porpoises; they ~~avrij~~ average five feet (1.5 meters) in ~~lenth~~ length. As their name ~~imply~~ implies, they ~~prefers~~ prefer to stay close to land rather than venture out into the open ocean visitors who are lucky enough to catch ~~cite~~ sight of the porpoises are likely to hear them, too. As the animal's exhale, they make a puffing sound. Long ago, ~~sailers~~ sailors used to call these porpoises "puffing pigs." The fact that these ~~creachures~~ creatures seem ~~comfterble~~ comfortable around boats in the bay ~~are~~ is a good sign. It means that researchers will be able to study the porpoises' social structure and life cycle. It is also a good sign for our environment.

Error Summary

Capitalization	1
Language Usage	4
Punctuation:	
Apostrophe	2
Period	1
Quotation Mark	1
Spelling	6

Name _____

WEDNESDAY   Week 22

What else besides water quality may have drove away the harbor porpoises. Many things was going on during the 1940s that might have frightened the shy animals. For one thing, the San Francisco Bay certainly was a busseling place. The US Navy put a underwater net across the entrunse to the bay. This net which was seven miles long was installed to prevent enemy submireens from entering the bay. In addition the millitery set hundreds of mines just outside the Golden Gate. All of this activity plus the water pollution caused by manufacturing and raw sewage made the bay a unfaverible place for porpoises to live.

- abbreviations
- verbs
- commas

THURSDAY   Week 22

Harbor porpoises are smaller then most porpoises; they avrij five feet (1.5 meters) in lenth. As their name imply, they prefers to stay close to land rather than venture out into the open ocean, visitors who are lucky enough to catch cite of the porpoises are likely to hear them, too. As the animal's exhale, they make a puffing sound. Long ago, sailers used to call these porpoises "puffing pigs. The fact that these creachures seem comfterble around boats in the bay are a good sign. It means that researchers will be able to study the porpoises social structure and life cycle. It is also a good sign for our environment.

- verbs
- apostrophes
- quotation marks

MONDAY   Week 23

Billy Fisher, Pony Express Rider

William f Fisher, better known as billy fisher, was born in 1839 in england. He died in 1919 in idaho, five weeks shy of his eightieth birthday. Between those two date's, he had an ~~exciteing~~ exciting life. The ~~hilight~~ highlight may have been the time he spent working for the pony express.

Before 1860 mail delivery was a slow process, taking 24 days between missouri and the West Coast. ~~Tenshunz~~ Tensions in the years before the Civil war made it ~~necesairy~~ necessary to speed up news delivery. ~~Ridders~~ Riders like Billy Fisher had to be prepared for long wearisome journeys.

Error Summary

Capitalization	9
Punctuation:	
Apostrophe	1
Comma	2
Period	1
Spelling	5

TUESDAY   Week 23

The entire Pony Express route ~~were~~ was almost 2,000 miles (3,220 kilometers) long. It stretched from St. Joseph Missouri, to sacramento california. Fisher, who rode mainly in nevada and utah was a fearless ~~deddecated~~ dedicated rider. He once covered 300 miles (482.8 kilometers) in 30 hours. This was ~~incredible~~ incredibly fast, considering that he also switched horses at several ~~stayshuns~~ stations along the way.

The pony express was in business for only 18 months. The nation no longer needed it after the transcontinental ~~tellegraf~~ telegraph was developed. However stories of brave and ~~darring~~ daring riders like fisher persist even today.

Error Summary

Capitalization	7
Language Usage	2
Punctuation:	
Comma	5
Period	1
Spelling	4

Name _____

Billy Fisher, Pony Express Rider

William f Fisher, better known as billy fisher, was born in 1839 in england. He died in 1919 in idaho, five weeks shy of his eightieth birthday. Between those two date's, he had an exciteing life. The hilight may have been the time he spent working for the pony express.

Before 1860 mail delivery was a slow process, taking 24 days between missouri and the West Coast. Tenshunz in the years before the Civil war made it necesairy to speed up news delivery. Ridders like Billy Fisher had to be prepared for long wearisome journeys.

- personal names
- place names
- company names
- historic events

The entire Pony Express route were almost 2,000 miles (3,220 kilometers) long. It stretched from St Joseph Missouri, to sacramento california. Fisher, who rode mainly in nevada and utah was a fearless deddecated rider. He once covered 300 miles (482.8 kilometers) in 30 hours. This was incredible fast, considering that he also switched horses at several stayshuns along the way.

The pony express was in business for only 18 months. The nation no longer needed it after the transcontinental tellegraf was developed. However stories of brave and darring riders like fisher persist even today.

- abbreviations
- place names
- commas
- adverbs

WEDNESDAY　　　　Week 23

One dramatic story from Fisher's Pony Express days
describes
~~describe~~ a time when he ~~all most~~ almost died. It was a cold winter

day in January 1861. Fisher lost his way during a ~~seveer~~ severe

snow storm. Exhausted and chilled to the bone, he climbed
horse　　　collapsed
down from his ~~hoarse~~ and ~~collapse~~ on a clearing that was

some what protected by trees. He propped ~~hisself~~ himself up against

a tree trunk and huddled against the cold wind. He later
admitted
~~admited~~ that he had been tempted to start a fire using the

united states mail to stay warm, but he couldn't bring himself

to do it. Instead, he just rested on the ground and waited

for the storm to end.

Error Summary

Capitalization	2
Language Usage	3
Punctuation:	
Apostrophe	2
Spelling	6

THURSDAY　　　　Week 23

Meanwhile, Fisher began to fall asleep—that is, until he

felt something jump on his legs and lick his face. At first, he

didn't realize what was happening, nor did he realize how close

he was to freezing. He felt the licking again, so he opened
staring
his eyes. A rabbit was ~~stairing~~ into his face! Fisher's startled

reaction, caused the rabbit to scamper away. Fisher said,

"that the rabbit had saved his life." If the rabbit hadn't

awakened him, fisher might have died from the cold. As it

was, he got up, and started moving around. He ~~than~~ then noticed
cabin　　　　　　　refuge
a light in a nearby ~~cabbin~~, where he sought ~~refyooge~~ from

the cold. The next day, Fisher resumed his journey.

Error Summary

Capitalization	1
Language Usage	1
Punctuation:	
Apostrophe	2
Comma	6
Quotation Mark	2
Spelling	3

Name _____

WEDNESDAY   Week 23

One dramatic story from Fishers Pony Express days describe a time when he all most died. It was a cold winter day in January 1861. Fisher lost his way during a seveer snow storm. Exhausted and chilled to the bone, he climbed down from his hoarse and collapse on a clearing that was some what protected by trees. He propped hisself up against a tree trunk and huddled against the cold wind. He later admited that he had been tempted to start a fire using the united states mail to stay warm, but he couldnt bring himself to do it. Instead, he just rested on the ground and waited for the storm to end.

- verbs
- apostrophes
- compound words

THURSDAY   Week 23

Meanwhile, Fisher began to fall asleep—that is, until he felt something jump on his legs and lick his face. At first, he didnt realize what was happening nor did he realize how close he was to freezing. He felt the licking again so he opened his eyes. A rabbit was stairing into his face! Fisher's startled reaction, caused the rabbit to scamper away. Fisher said, "that the rabbit had saved his life." If the rabbit hadnt awakened him fisher might have died from the cold. As it was, he got up, and started moving around. He than noticed a light in a nearby cabbin, where he sought refyooge from the cold. The next day, Fisher resumed his journey.

- run-on sentences
- commas
- quotation marks

MONDAY   Week 24

Balto

Visitors to central Park in New York City can admire
the bronze statue of balto, a siberian husky sled dog. Beneath
the statue is a plaque with the following inscription: "Dedicated
to the indomitable spirit of the sled dogs that relayed
antitoxin six hundred miles over rough ice across treacherous
waters through icy blizzards from Nenana to the relief of
stricken Nome in the Winter of 1925." The statue was placed
there on december 17, 1925, less than a year after the real
husky's heroic race to nome, alaska. Why did the story of
this race capture the hearts of New Yorkers?

Error Summary

Capitalization	7
Punctuation:	
Apostrophe	1
Comma	2
Question Mark	1
Quotation Mark	2
Spelling	9

TUESDAY   Week 24

In january 1925, the city of Nome faced an outbreak
of diphtheria, an infectious bacterial disease that often
was fatal. The disease had killed one child already, and
other children were ill. If Nome's doctor didn't receive the
lifesaving serum immediately, the consequences would be
dire. Serum was available in anchorage, which was about
1,000 miles (1,610 kilometers) away, but making the journey
by airplane wasn't an option. So officials put the serum on
a train headed for nenana, the last stop on the line. Sled
Dogs would take the serum the rest of the way, which was
a distance of about 650 miles (1,046 kilometers).

Error Summary

Capitalization	4
Language Usage	3
Punctuation:	
Comma	4
Parentheses	1
Spelling	5

Name _____

Balto

Visiters to central Park in New York City can admier the bronze statue of balto a siberian husky sled dog. Beneth the statue is a plack with the following inscription: Dedicated to the indomitable spirrit of the sled dogs that relayed antitoxin six hunderd miles over rough ice across trecherous waters through icy blizards from Nenana to the releif of stricken Nome in the Winter of 1925". The statue was placed there on december 17 1925, less than a year after the real huskys heroic race to nome, alaska. Why did the story of this race capture the hearts of New Yorkers

WATCH FOR

- place names
- quotation marks
- dates

In january 1925, the city of Nome faced a outbrake of diphtheria a infectious bacterial disease that often was fatel. The disease have killed one child already and other children were ill. If Nome's docter didn't recieve the lifesaving serum immediately, the consequenses would be dire. Serum was available in anchorage, which was about 1,000 miles (1,610 kilometers) away but making the journey by airplane wasn't an option. So officials put the serum on a train headed for nenana, the last stop on the line. Sled Dogs would take the serum the rest of the way which was a distance of about 650 miles (1,046 kilometers.

WATCH FOR

- place names
- commas
- parentheses

WEDNESDAY   Week 24

More ~~then~~ than 20 mushers (dog sled drivers) and 100 dogs took part in the relay race; the first musher left Nenana just before midnight on january 27. The serum was ~~dellivered~~ delivered to Nome on ~~Febuary~~ February 2 at 530 in the morning. The teams had covered ~~aproximately~~ approximately 650 miles in about five and ~~an~~ a half days; this was a record-setting time. Balto was the dog leading the last team, and norwegian-born gunnar kaasen was the musher. Kaasen said that whiteout conditions on the trail made it almost impossible for him to see; however Balto was always able to keep to the ~~trial~~ trail, even after strong winds flipped the sled over.

Error Summary

Capitalization	7
Language Usage	2
Punctuation:	
Colon	1
Comma	2
Parentheses	1
Period	3
Spelling	4

THURSDAY   Week 24

Called the "Great Race of Mercy," the event was big news. Although five people died from diphtheria that winter in Nome, the death toll would have been much ~~worst~~ worse without the serum. Kaasen and balto did their part, but musher leonhard seppala and his lead dog, Togo, ~~is~~ are widely believed to be the genuine ~~heros~~ heroes. They transported the serum 91 miles (146 kilometers), the single ~~farther~~ farthest distance of any team. They also traveled over the ~~dangerousest~~ most dangerous part of the route. Balto got most of the glory, though, because he was the one that reached the goal. The statue in Central Park commemorates his ~~acheivemunt~~ achievement.

Error Summary

Capitalization	3
Language Usage	4
Punctuation:	
Comma	2
Quotation Mark	1
Spelling	2

Name _____

WEDNESDAY   Week 24

More then 20 mushers (dog sled drivers and 100 dogs took part in the relay race, the first musher left Nenana just before midnight on january 27. The serum was dellivered to Nome on Febuary 2 at 530 in the morning. The teams had covered aproximately 650 miles in about five and an half days, this was a record-setting time. Balto was the dog leading the last team and norwegian-born gunnar kaasen was the musher. Kaasen said that whiteout conditions on the trail made it almost impossible for him to see, however Balto was always able to keep to the trial, even after strong winds flipped the sled over.

- parentheses
- time
- run-on sentences
- nationalities

THURSDAY   Week 24

Called the "Great Race of Mercy, the event was big news. Although five people died from diphtheria that winter in Nome, the death toll would have been much worst without the serum. Kaasen and balto did their part but musher leonhard seppala and his lead dog, Togo, is widely believed to be the genuine heros. They transported the serum 91 miles (146 kilometers), the single farther distance of any team. They also traveled over the dangerousest part of the route. Balto got most of the glory, though because he was the one that reached the goal. The statue in Central Park commemorates his acheivemunt.

- quotation marks
- words that compare

The Mystery of the Space Rocks

Liam read the ad again. "For a ~~meer~~ (mere) $49.95 including tax," Liam read aloud, "You can enroll in our online science ~~coarse~~ (course). This sum also ~~entitels~~ (entitles) you to a rock from Saturn. We'll send you this rock by ~~reguler~~ (regular) mail and provide an online worksheet on the ~~phisicle~~ (physical) properties of rocks. One of the lessons will help you identify rocks and minerals."

"I have just enough money to do this," said Liam, checking his ~~wollit~~ (wallet). Then he got ~~permishion~~ (permission) from his Mom to charge the enrollment fee to her credit card. He gave her $50 to cover the charge. "Keep the change," he told her.

Capitalization	3
Punctuation:	
Period	2
Quotation Mark	3
Spelling	7

Liam looked ~~foreword~~ (forward) to showing the rock to Adam, his best ~~freind~~ (friend). He checked the mail every day for ~~fore~~ (four) weeks, but nothing had arrived. On the twenty-ninth day, he checked the mail again, still there was nothing. Liam was enjoying his online science lessons, but he was ~~begining~~ (beginning) to feel that he ~~was'nt~~ (wasn't) getting his money's worth. Most of the ~~lessins~~ (lessons) were full of information that was ~~avalible~~ (available) online for free. Why had he been such a fool to pay $49.95? If only that rock would ~~arive~~ (arrive) he wouldn't feel so cheated. He wanted to ~~suprise~~ (surprise) his friend. Adam was crazy about ~~geologie~~ (geology) and Liam knew that the rock from Saturn would amaze him.

Punctuation:	
Apostrophe	2
Comma	3
Hyphen	2
Period	1
Question Mark	1
Spelling	10

Name ————————————————————————

The Mystery of the Space Rocks

Liam read the ad again. "For a meer $49.95 including tax, Liam read aloud, "You can enroll in our online science coarse. This sum also entitels you to a rock from Saturn. We'll send you this rock by reguler mail and provide an online worksheet on the phisicle properties of rocks, one of the lessons will help you identify rocks and minerals."

"I have just enough money to do this", said Liam, checking his wollit. Then he got permishion from his Mom to charge the enrollment fee to her credit card. He gave her $50 to cover the charge. "Keep the change, he told her

- dialogue
- run-on sentences

Liam looked foreword to showing the rock to Adam his best freind. He checked the mail every day for fore weeks, but nothing had arrived. On the twenty ninth-day, he checked the mail again, still there was nothing. Liam was enjoying his online science lessons, but he was begining to feel that he was'nt getting his moneys worth. Most of the lessins were full of information that was avalible online for free. Why had he been such a fool to pay $49.95. If only that rock would arive he wouldnt feel so cheated. He wanted to suprise his friend. Adam was crazy about geolegie and Liam knew that the rock from Saturn would amaze him.

- apostrophes
- hyphens
- run-on sentences

WEDNESDAY　　　　　　　　　　　　　　Week 25

Finally, the ~~packedge~~ *package* arrived. Liam ~~tears~~ *tore* open the box, and admired the rock. It was larger than he had expected. it looked a lot like rocks he saw all the time, but he was sure that hed be able to prove that it was special. After all it was from Saturn so it had to be ~~differant~~ *different* from Earth rocks. He went online to get the worksheet, then he hurried over to Adams house to share his ~~excitment~~ *excitement*.

"Liam, somebodys tricking you," said Adam, after he ~~herd~~ *heard* the story. "That rock cant be from Saturn, but we can still have fun testing the physical properties and figuring out what kind of rock it is."

Error Summary

Capitalization	2
Language Usage	1
Punctuation:	
Apostrophe	4
Comma	4
Period	3
Quotation Mark	2
Spelling	4

THURSDAY　　　　　　　　　　　　　　Week 25

"How do you know its not from Saturn" asked liam.

"Well, that's no mystery," said Adam. "Saturn is a gas giant, like jupiter and neptune. Its mostly Hydrogen and Helium. Even if Saturns core is made of solid rock, we ~~would'nt~~ *wouldn't* have ~~no~~ *any* rocks from there. No spaceship ~~have~~ *has* ever traveled there and back. Let's read the ad again."

Liam quickly found the ad. "Saturn Science Education," he read aloud, "offers a special course. Study rocks from around the World. Well send you one each month."

"See, Liam? Saturn is the name of the company, not the ~~planit~~ *planet* where the rock comes from!" explained Adam.

Error Summary

Capitalization	6
Language Usage	2
Punctuation:	
Apostrophe	5
Question Mark	1
Quotation Mark	5
Spelling	2

Name _____

WEDNESDAY   Week 25

Finally, the packedge arrived. Liam tears open the box, and admired the rock. It was larger than he had expected, it looked a lot like rocks he saw all the time, but he was sure that hed be able to prove that it was special. After all it was from Saturn so it had to be differant from Earth rocks. He went online to get the worksheet, then he hurried over to Adams house to share his excitment.

"Liam somebodys tricking you, said Adam, after he herd the story. "That rock cant be from Saturn, but we can still have fun testing the physical properties and figuring out what kind of rock it is

WATCH FOR

- verbs
- apostrophes
- dialogue

THURSDAY   Week 25

"How do you know its not from Saturn" asked liam.

"Well, that's no mystery, said Adam. Saturn is a gas giant, like jupiter and neptune. Its mostly Hydrogen and Helium. Even if Saturns' core is made of solid rock, we would'nt have no rocks from there. No spaceship have ever traveled there and back. Lets read the ad again."

Liam quickly found the ad. "Saturn Science Education, he read aloud, offers a special course. Study rocks from around the World. Well send you one each month."

"See, Liam? Saturn is the name of the company, not the planit where the rock comes from! explained Adam.

WATCH FOR

- apostrophes
- dialogue
- names of planets

MONDAY	Week 26

Error Summary

Language Usage	3
Punctuation:	
Apostrophe	1
Comma	1
Hyphen	1
Spelling	12

Pecos Bill Rides a Tornado

It is common ~~knollege~~ knowledge that Pecos Bill was quite ~~a~~ an ~~acommplished~~ accomplished rider. Not a bronco alive could throw him. In fact, I knew of only one time in Bills ~~profeshunal~~ professional life when he had been ~~throwed~~ thrown. I'd heard the ~~storey~~ story from an old-timer who'd ~~witnist~~ witnessed the event with his own eyes. He told me that Pecos Bill had simply ~~desided~~ decided one day to ride a ~~tornadoe~~ tornado. Bill had ~~got~~ gotten the ~~riddiculus~~ ridiculous notion while visiting ~~frends~~ friends in the state of Kansas. Not one of Bill's side kicks could talk him out of the idea. That was an other well-known thing about Pecos Bill: He was as ~~stuborn~~ stubborn as a mule.

TUESDAY	Week 26

Error Summary

Language Usage	4
Punctuation:	
Apostrophe	2
Comma	7
Spelling	4

As every one knew, Pecos Bill could not be stopped once he got an idea. Further more, Bill wasn't planning to ride just any little tornado. He let the small ones go ~~buy~~ by, and he waited for the ~~gigantickest~~ most gigantic tornado any one had ever ~~saw~~ seen. As the twister neared Kansas, the sky turned purple and black. The tornado bellowed so loudly that it woke up babies on the other side of the world! Bill acted ~~prompt~~ promptly. He grabbed that surly tornado, slammed it to the ground, and hopped right on it's back. The tornado bucked, and kicked, and yelled ~~conspicuous~~ conspicuously enough to be heard all the way in Texas. No matter what that tornado did, Bill held on.

Name _____

Pecos Bill Rides a Tornado

It is common knollege that Pecos Bill was quite a acommplished rider. Not a bronco alive could throw him. In fact I knew of only one time in Bills profeshunal life when he had been throwed. I'd heard the storey from an old-timer who'd witnist the event with his own eyes. He told me that Pecos Bill had simply desided one day to ride a tornadoe. Bill had got the riddiculus notion while visiting frends in the state of Kansas. Not one of Bill's side kicks could talk him out of the idea. That was an other well known thing about Pecos Bill: He was as stuborn as a mule.

- verbs
- compound words
- hyphens

As every one knew, Pecos Bill could not be stopped once he got an idea. Further more, Bill wasnt planning to ride just any little tornado. He let the small ones go buy and he waited for the gigantickest tornado any one had ever saw. As the twister neared Kansas the sky turned purple and black. The tornado bellowed so loudly that it woke up babies on the other side of the world! Bill acted prompt. He grabbed that surly tornado slammed it to the ground and hopped right on it's back. The tornado bucked, and kicked, and yelled conspicuous enough to be heard all the way in Texas. No matter what that tornado did Bill held on.

- commas
- compound words
- words that compare
- adverbs

WEDNESDAY   Week 26

as that angry tornado ~~tryed~~ tried to throw Bill off its' back it churned up the local rivers and tied them into knots. No ~~forrest~~ forest was safe from the fury of that tornado, either. The twister flattened all of the forests in one spot along the ~~boarder~~ border between Texas and new mexico, turning the trees into tooth picks that ~~blue~~ blew out to sea. Folks renamed the area the "Staked Plains" and ~~lammented~~ lamented the loss of 30,000 square miles of prime timber land. This didn't bother Bill at all, though. He continued riding that tornado, and stayed as calm as a june day. Every now and then, he'd give it a jab with his sharp spurs.

Error Summary

Capitalization	4
Punctuation:	
Apostrophe	2
Comma	2
Period	1
Quotation Mark	1
Spelling	7

THURSDAY   Week 26

At last, that wily tornado figured out that it wasn't ~~never~~ ever going to get pecos Bill off it's back. It had ~~ran~~ run out of tricks and nothing had worked, that's when it headed over to california and rained itself out. There was so much rain that it filled the grand canyon, way over in Arizona. When the tornado ~~wownd~~ wound down to ~~practikly~~ practically nothing, Bill fell off. He must ~~of~~ have let his attention slip, for just a second. He hit the ground with so much force, that he sank below sea level. People named that place "death valley". Anyway, it was the tornado that gave folk's the idea for the Rodeo. These days, however, most cowboys prefer to ride bronco's.

Error Summary

Capitalization	9
Language Usage	3
Punctuation:	
Apostrophe	4
Comma	1
Period	2
Quotation Mark	2
Spelling	2

Name _____

WEDNESDAY	Week 26

- compound words
- special words in quotation marks

as that angry tornado tryed to throw Bill off its' back it churned up the local rivers and tied them into knots. No forrest was safe from the fury of that tornado, either. The twister flattened all of the forests in one spot along the boarder between Texas and new mexico, turning the trees into tooth picks that blue out to sea. Folks renamed the area the "Staked Plains and lammented the loss of 30,000 square miles of prime timber land. This didnt bother Bill at all, though. He continued riding that tornado, and stayed as calm as a june day. Every now and then, he'd give it a jab with his sharp spurs

THURSDAY	Week 26

- place names
- run-on sentences
- incomplete sentences

At last, that wily tornado figured out that it wasn't never going to get pecos Bill off it's back. It had ran out of tricks and nothing had worked, thats when it headed over to california and rained itself out. There was so much rain that it filled the grand canyon, way over in Arizona. When the tornado wownd down to practikly nothing, Bill fell off. He must of let his attention slip, for just a second. He hit the ground with so much force. That he sank below sea level. People named that place death valley". Anyway, it was the tornado that gave folk's the idea for the Rodeo. These days, however, most cowboys prefer to ride bronco's.

MONDAY Week 27

Chasing Twisters

Joshua Wurman is a ~~wether~~ weather scientist who studies twisters, or tornadoes. What, precisely, are tornadoes, and where does Wurman go to find them? A tornado is a ~~colum~~ column of fast-spinning air that ~~stretch~~ stretches from the ground to storm clouds above. Tornadoes can pack winds of up to 300 miles (483 kilometers) per hour. When they hit a populated area, they can be devastating. Tornadoes ~~occurs~~ occur on every ~~contenent~~ continent ~~accept~~ except antarctica. Most, however, occur in the United States in ~~a~~ an area named "Tornado Alley," Which ~~cover~~ covers northern Texas and much of oklahoma, kansas, nebraska, and south dakota.

Error Summary

Capitalization	7
Language Usage	4
Punctuation:	
Comma	6
Parentheses	1
Question Mark	1
Quotation Mark	1
Spelling	4

TUESDAY Week 27

Wurmans work ~~take~~ takes him on the ~~rode~~ road a lot. We catch up with him for this Interview to learn more about his job.

Q: How did you become interested, in studying storms?

A: Tornadoes always ~~repressented~~ represented the unknown to me. They're a mystery of Nature. I wanted to see what was behind that mystery in order to find out how tornadoes worked.

Q: How ~~do~~ does it feel to see a twister at close range?

A: It's exciting, but also ~~hecktick~~ hectic. While I'm there, I have to ~~jugle~~ juggle teams of people in various ~~vehicals~~ vehicles all around the tornado. I have to make sure the team's can get in and out of the area safely.

Error Summary

Capitalization	2
Language Usage	2
Punctuation:	
Apostrophe	5
Comma	2
Period	1
Question Mark	2
Spelling	5

Name _____

Chasing Twisters

Joshua Wurman is a wether scientist who studies twisters or tornadoes. What, precisely, are tornadoes, and where does Wurman go to find them. A tornado is a colum of fast-spinning air that stretch from the ground to storm clouds above. Tornadoes can pack winds of up to 300 miles (483) kilometers per hour. When they hit a populated area, they can be devastating. Tornadoes occurs on every contenent accept antarctica. Most however, occur in the United States in a area named "Tornado Alley. Which cover northern Texas and much of oklahoma kansas nebraska and south dakota.

- parentheses
- place names
- special words in quotation marks

Wurmans work take him on the rode a lot. We catch up with him for this Interview to learn more about his job.

Q: How did you become interested, in studying storms

A: Tornadoes always repressented the unknown to me. Theyre a mystery of Nature. I wanted to see what was behind that mystery in order to find out how tornadoes worked.

Q: How do it feel to see a twister at close range

A: Its exciting, but also hecktick. While Im there, I have to jugle teams of people in various vehicals all around the tornado? I have to make sure the team's can get in and out of the area safely.

- apostrophes
- verbs

WEDNESDAY   Week 27

Q: Obviously, chasing twisters is dangerous work. How do you
make sure that you and your ~~crue~~ crew stay safe?

A: Our ~~moble~~ mobile radar trucks ~~is a~~ are an effective safety tool.

Q: ~~Your'e~~ You're talking about Doppler on Wheels or DOWs, right?

A: That's correct. With this ~~equipmunt~~ equipment, we can tell how big
the tornado is, how strong it is, and ~~weather~~ whether it's getting more
~~intents~~ intense. We can also measure the wind speed, and direction.

We place the dow trucks so they have different views of
the tornado. The idea is to get them as close as possible
(about two or three miles away) so we can collect data as the
twister moves. As you know, the tornado is a moving target.

Error Summary

Capitalization	3
Language Usage	2
Punctuation:	
Apostrophe	2
Comma	6
Parentheses	1
Spelling	6

THURSDAY   Week 27

Q: ~~Ultamately~~ Ultimately, what do you ~~ikspeck~~ expect to learn?

A: We hope to find out more about the structure of
tornadoes and how they ~~forms~~ form; then we can get better at
~~fourcasting~~ forecasting them. The average ~~leed~~ lead time ~~currantly~~ currently is less
than 15 minutes. Which ~~does'nt~~ doesn't give people in the area much
time to prepare. Also, more than half of the warnings ~~is~~ are
false alarms. we need to predict with greater accuracy.

Q: what advice do you have for anyone who ~~are~~ interested
in chasing tornadoes?

A: My advice is to find an ~~expeariensed~~ experienced partner and to learn
about storms first. Tornadoes are ~~fassinating~~ fascinating but dangerous.

Error Summary

Capitalization	3
Language Usage	3
Punctuation:	
Comma	1
Period	2
Question Mark	2
Spelling	8

Name _____

WEDNESDAY   Week 27

- commas
- apostrophes

Q: Obviously chasing twisters is dangerous work. How do you make sure that you and your crue stay safe?

A: Our moble radar trucks is a effective safety tool.

Q: Your'e talking about Doppler on Wheels or DOWs right?

A: Thats correct. With this equipmunt, we can tell how big the tornado is, how strong it is and weather its getting more intents. We can also measure the wind speed, and direction. We place the dow trucks so they have different views of the tornado. The idea is to get them as close as possible about two or three miles away) so we can collect data as the twister moves. As you know the tornado is a moving target.

THURSDAY   Week 27

- end punctuation
- incomplete sentences
- run-on sentences

Q: Ultamately, what do you ikspeck to learn

A: We hope to find out more about the structure of tornadoes and how they forms; then we can get better at fourcasting them. The average leed time currantly is less than 15 minutes. Which does'nt give people in the area much time to prepare. Also, more than half of the warnings is false alarms, we need to predict with greater accuracy.

Q: what advice do you have for anyone who are interested in chasing tornadoes

A: My advice is to find an expeariensed partner and to learn about storms first. Tornadoes are fassinating but dangerous

MONDAY   Week 28

The Community Garden

It was a sad day in my neighborhood when the
nineteenth-century Pettigrew ~~Appartments~~ *Apartments* were ~~tore~~ *torn* down.
Two city officials wearing suits and carrying clip_boards had
~~came~~ *come* by. "This *A*partment building is unsafe," they said. "To
protect the ~~residants~~ *residents*, we have to demolish it."

Within a few months, all of the residents had ~~move~~ *moved*
to other buildings. A crane with a ~~recking~~ *wrecking* ball arrived one
~~mourning~~ *morning*. By noon that day, the old-fashioned building had
been ~~knock~~ *knocked* to the ground. Worker's took the rubble away in
trucks and ~~leaved~~ *left* an empty lot in the middle of the block.

Error Summary

Capitalization	2
Language Usage	5
Punctuation:	
Apostrophe	1
Comma	2
Hyphen	2
Quotation Mark	2
Spelling	5

TUESDAY   Week 28

A year later, the lot had ~~became~~ *become* ~~a~~ *an* eyesore, full of
weeds and trash. Former resident's came by and stared
~~sorroefully~~ *sorrowfully* at the space. "At one time, that building could ~~of~~ *have*
been saved," said Mrs. O'Leary, "but no one even tried."

"I feel ~~terrible~~ *terribly* melancholy to see this empty lot," said
Mr. Jameson. "My kids grew up at the old Pettigrew. We
were proud of the place. Now there's nothing here to give us
pride. Our old home is just ~~a~~ *an* ugly, vacant, city lot."

That's when the idea ~~come~~ *came* to me. We could transform
that ~~eyesoar~~ *eyesore* into a place that neighbors could call their own.
A ~~comunity~~ *community* garden ~~seamed~~ *seemed* like the perfect place.

Error Summary

Language Usage	6
Punctuation:	
Apostrophe	3
Comma	2
Period	2
Quotation Mark	5
Spelling	4

Name _____

The Community Garden

It was a sad day in my neighborhood when the nineteenth century Pettigrew Appartments were tore down. Two city officials wearing suits and carrying clip boards had came by. "This Apartment building is unsafe" they said. to protect the residants, we have to demolish it".

Within a few months, all of the residents had move to other buildings. A crane with a recking ball arrived one mourning. By noon that day the old fashioned building had been knock to the ground. Worker's took the rubble away in trucks and leaved an empty lot in the middle of the block.

- names of buildings
- verbs
- hyphens
- compound words

A year later, the lot had became a eyesore, full of weeds and trash. Former resident's came by and stared sorroefully at the space. "At one time that building could of been saved, said Mrs O'Leary, but no one even tried.

"I feel terrible melancholy to see this empty lot, said Mr Jameson. "My kids grew up at the old Pettigrew. We were proud of the place. Now theres nothing here to give us pride. Our old home is just a ugly, vacant, city lot.

Thats when the idea come to me. We could transform that eyesoar into a place that neighbors could call their own. A comunity garden seamed like the perfect place.

- verbs
- abbreviations
- dialogue

WEDNESDAY　　　　　　　　　　　　　　　Week 28

　　　　My friend lisa and ~~me~~ (I) went to see ~~mr~~ Green, who ~~use~~ (used) to work for the city. We thought he might have some inside information concerning city policies, about vacant lots. "there was a program," he said, "that let people rent ~~emfey~~ (empty) lots belonging to the city. I'm not sure if it's still in place, but you could ~~inkwire~~ (inquire) at the city offices." So that's how it all ~~come~~ (came) about. Lisa and I learned that we needed to collect a hundred ~~signiturs~~ (signatures) on a petition. With that and one dollar, we could rent the lot if we ~~prommised~~ (promised) to improve it. Getting the signatures ~~were~~ (was) easy. Everyone in the neighbor hood was sick of seeing that weedy, trash-filled lot.

Error Summary

Capitalization	3
Language Usage	4
Punctuation:	
Apostrophe	3
Comma	5
Period	2
Quotation Mark	2
Spelling	5

THURSDAY　　　　　　　　　　　　　　　Week 28

　　　　within two weeks, we had rented the lot from the city. The next saturday, Lisa and ~~me~~ (I) started picking up the trash, putting it in bags, and carrying it to the ~~cerb~~ (curb). When neighbors ~~seen~~ (saw) what we were doing, they offered to help. Everyone seemed to have at least ~~a~~ (an) hour to ~~spair~~ (spare). Friends called friends, and very soon the lot was cleared and ready for planting. ~~Us~~ (We) all shared ideas about what to plant. By that summer, we had a ~~thriveing~~ (thriving) garden with flowers, and vegetables, of all kinds. Today, we even have a few benches ~~wear~~ (where) people can ~~set~~ (sit) and enjoy the view. Now all we need ~~are~~ (is) a name for the place. I'm going to ~~sugest~~ (suggest) "New memories."

Error Summary

Capitalization	4
Language Usage	6
Punctuation:	
Comma	6
Quotation Mark	1
Spelling	5

Name _____

My friend lisa and me went to see mr Green who use to work for the city. We thought he might have some inside information concerning city policies, about vacant lots. "there was a program, he said, that let people rent emtey lots belonging to the city. Im not sure if its still in place but you could inkwire at the city offices" So thats how it all come about. Lisa and I learned that we needed to collect a hundred signiturs on a petition. With that and one dollar we could rent the lot if we prommised to improve it. Getting the signatures were easy. Everyone in the neighbor hood was sick of seeing that weedy trash-filled lot.

- pronouns
- dialogue
- place names

within two weeks we had rented the lot from the City. The next saturday, Lisa and me started picking up the trash putting it in bags and carrying it to the cerb. When neighbors seen what we were doing they offered to help. Everyone seemed to have at least a hour to spair. Friends called friends, and very soon the lot was cleared and ready for planting. Us all shared ideas about what to plant. By that summer, we had a thriveing garden with flowers, and vegetables, of all kinds. Today, we even have a few benches wear people can set and enjoy the view. Now all we need are a name for the place. I'm going to sugest "New memories".

- verbs
- commas

MONDAY   **Week 29**

Time to Sleep

Everyone needs a certain amount of sleep ~~daylie~~ [daily] but some people ~~requires~~ [require] more ~~then~~ [than] others. Whereas some ~~helthy~~ [healthy] adults don't need ~~no~~ [any] more than six hours of sleep others aren't at their best unless they ~~gets~~ [get] ten or even twelve hours. Actually our sleep requirements ~~changes~~ [change] as we ~~matoor~~ [mature]. Babies need about eighteen hours of sleep a day. Most children by age 10 sleep only nine to ten hours per night most teenagers sleep about nine hours—~~slitely~~ [slightly] more than the average for adults. No matter what your age, it's important to get an adequate amount of sleep on a regular ~~bases~~ [basis].

Error Summary

Capitalization	1
Language Usage	5
Punctuation:	
Apostrophe	3
Comma	3
Period	1
Spelling	5

TUESDAY   **Week 29**

Sleep ~~give~~ [gives] us a chance to rest our bodies and recover from daily stress It also gives our brains time to dream, which is one way that brains process the information that we ~~acquires~~ [acquire] during ~~wakeing~~ [waking] hours. You may be surprised, to learn that our minds remain active as we sleep. How do we know this? In ~~S~~sleep ~~S~~studies patients are attached to ~~insterments~~ [instruments] that measure brain activity as well as breathing, heart rate, and muscle movements These studies ~~analyzes~~ [analyze] a pattern that ~~alternate~~ [alternates] between two ~~mane~~ [main] types of sleep: rapid eye movement (REM) and non-REM sleep. A typical cycle lasts roughly ~~ninty~~ [ninety] minutes and repeats five times a night.

Error Summary

Capitalization	2
Language Usage	4
Punctuation:	
Comma	5
Period	2
Question Mark	1
Spelling	4

Name _____

MONDAY   Week 29

Time to Sleep

Everyone needs a certain amount of sleep daylie but some people requires more then others. Whereas some helthy adults dont need no more than six hours of sleep others arent at their best unless they gets ten or even twelve hours. Actually our sleep requirements changes as we matoor. Babies need about eighteen hours of sleep a day. Most children by age 10 sleep only nine to ten hours per night, most teenagers sleep about nine hours—slitely more than the average for adults. No matter what your age, its important to get an adequate amount of sleep on a regular bases.

- commas
- verbs
- run-on sentences

TUESDAY   Week 29

Sleep give us a chance to rest our bodies and recover from daily stress It also gives our brains time to dream which is one way that brains process the information that we acquires during wakeing hours. You may be surprised, to learn that our minds remain active as we sleep. How do we know this. In Sleep Studies patients are attached to insturments that measure brain activity as well as breathing heart rate and muscle movements These studies analyzes a pattern that alternate between two mane types of sleep: rapid eye movement (REM) and non-REM sleep. A typical cycle lasts roughly ninty minutes and repeats five times a night.

- verbs
- end punctuation
- commas

WEDNESDAY　　　　　　　　　　　　　Week 29

Drowsiness is the first stage of non-REM sleep which

deepens ~~gradual~~ (gradually) during the sleep cycle. In the deep-sleep

stage of non-REM sleep, the body rests and ~~recharge~~ (recharges). This

is the time when the body ~~build~~ (builds) new muscle and bone tissue.

REM sleep is when people ~~experiants~~ (experience) dreams. This period

of sleep lasts about ten minutes at a time but lengthens

with ~~subsequint~~ (subsequent) sleep cycles. During rem sleep, most of the

muscles of the body ~~relaxes~~ (relax) but the heart rate and breathing

rise and fall ~~sudden~~ (suddenly). Also during REM sleep, the eyes make

short quick jerky movements these ~~distinktif~~ (distinctive) movements ~~gives~~ (give)

REM sleep its name.

Error Summary

Capitalization	4
Language Usage	6
Punctuation:	
Comma	5
Hyphen	1
Period	1
Spelling	3

THURSDAY　　　　　　　　　　　　　　Week 29

Some people ~~says~~ (say) that they never dream at night. The

fact is, everyone dreams during REM sleep but people dont

always remember ~~they're~~ (their) dreams. Remembering our dreams

can be ~~valuble~~ (valuable). Suppose you have a problem to solve the

solution just might ~~came~~ (come) to you in a dream. Thats why

people say theyll "sleep on it" when they have a problem

the solution may ~~surfuce~~ (surface) from the subconscious mind. Artists,

writers and other creative thinkers often get ideas from

their dreams. Wolfgang Mozart the famous ~~composor~~ (composer), for

example, claimed that all the music he wrote came to him

from his ~~dreems~~ (dreams). So being a dreamers a good thing!

Error Summary

Capitalization	2
Language Usage	2
Punctuation:	
Apostrophe	4
Comma	4
Period	2
Spelling	5

Name _____

WEDNESDAY   Week 29

• adverbs
• hyphens

   Drowsiness is the first stage of non-REM sleep which deepens gradual during the sleep cycle. In the deep-sleep stage of non REM sleep, the body rests and recharge. This is the time when the body build new muscle and bone tissue. REM sleep is when people experiants dreams. This period of sleep lasts about ten minutes at a time but lengthens, with subsequint sleep cycles. During rem sleep, most of the muscles of the body relaxes but the heart rate and breathing rise and fall sudden. Also during REM sleep, the eyes make short quick jerky movements, these distinktif movements gives REM sleep its name.

THURSDAY   Week 29

• apostrophes
• run-on sentences

   Some people says that they never dream at night. The fact is, everyone dreams during REM sleep but people dont always remember they're dreams. Remembering our dreams can be valuble. Suppose you have a problem to solve, the solution just might came to you in a dream. Thats why people say theyll "sleep on it" when they have a problem, the solution may surface from the subconscious mind. Artists, writers and other creative thinkers, often get ideas from their dreams. Wolfgang Mozart the famous composor, for example, claimed that all the music he wrote came to him from his dreems. So being a dreamers a good thing!

MONDAY   Week 30

A Royal Butterfly

The monarch is one of the largest, and colorfulest *most* butterflies. The wing span on this insect ~~are~~ *is* three to five inches ~~acceros~~ *across*. It's dazzling, orange and black wings ~~makes~~ *make* ~~them~~ *it* easy to see. You might think that the bright colors would ~~attracts~~ *attract* predators, and make the monarch easy ~~pray~~ *prey*. However, ~~predaters~~ *predators* know better than to feast on this butterfly. The ~~atractive~~ *attractive* colors serve as a warning, not an invitation, to predators. ~~l~~*L*ike a flashing red light at a corner, the colors scream, "Stop! *D*anger!" You may wonder what's so dangerous about this butterfly? Its, body is ~~poisinous~~ *poisonous*!

Error Summary

Capitalization	2
Language Usage	5
Punctuation:	
Apostrophe	3
Comma	5
Period	1
Quotation Mark	1
Spelling	6

TUESDAY   Week 30

What makes monarch butterflies poisonous? The answer lies in ~~there~~ *their* diet. Monarchs feed exclusively on a common, *flowering* ~~flowerring~~ plant known as milkweed, it is no coincidence that these insects are also called milkweed butterflies. Many species of milkweed ~~contains~~ *contain* ~~substinces~~ *substances* that are ~~toksick~~ *toxic* to most animals, but not to monarchs. In fact, the life of a ~~m~~*M*onarch ~~b~~*B*utterfly actually begins on a milkweed plant. Adult monarchs ~~lays~~ *lay* eggs on the plants. About four days later, the eggs hatch to reveal larvae, or ~~caterpillers~~ *caterpillars*. These colorful worm~-like creatures, continue to live on the milkweed, feeding on it for about ~~too~~ *two* weeks.

Error Summary

Capitalization	3
Language Usage	2
Punctuation:	
Comma	5
Hyphen	1
Period	1
Question Mark	1
Spelling	6

Name _____

- verbs
- commas
- words that compare

A Royal Butterfly

The monarch is one of the largest, and colorfulest butterflies. The wing span on this insect are three to five inches accros. It's dazzling, orange and black wings makes them easy to see. You might think that the bright colors would attracts predators, and make the monarch easy pray. However, predaters know better than to feast on this butterfly. The atractive colors serve as a warning not an invitation to predators. like a flashing red light at a corner, the colors scream, Stop! danger!" You may wonder whats so dangerous about this butterfly? Its' body is poisinous!

- end punctuation
- commas

What makes monarch butterflies poisonous. The answer lies in there diet. Monarchs feed exclusively on a common, flowerring, plant known as milkweed, it is no coincidence that these insects are also called milkweed butterflies. Many species of milkweed contains substinces that are toksick to most animals, but not to monarchs. In fact, the life of a Monarch Butterfly actually begins on a milkweed plant. Adult monarchs lays eggs on the plants. About four days later, the eggs hatch to reveal larvae or caterpillers. These colorful worm like creatures, continue to live on the milkweed, feeding on it for about too weeks.

WEDNESDAY   Week 30

Error Summary

Capitalization	2
Language Usage	3
Punctuation:	
Apostrophe	2
Comma	6
Parentheses	2
Period	1
Spelling	5

After two weeks, each plump caterpillar is approximately
two ~~inchs~~ (inches) long, and fully grown. It stops eating and then
spins a sticky, silk ~~thred~~ (thread) which it uses to ~~fastens~~ (fasten) it self,
hanging inverted, to a stem or a leaf. It ~~shed~~ (sheds) it's skin
of black, white, and yellow stripes and becomes a chrysalis
(also called a pupa). This is the next stage of the monarch's
life cycle. The shell around the pupa ~~grajally~~ (gradually) hardens and
becomes opaque. Inside the shell, the body of the former
caterpillar transforms into a butterfly. From the out side, it
~~look~~ (looks) as if nothing is taking place, the metamorphosis (which
means a "change in form") occurs in less than two weeks.

THURSDAY   Week 30

Error Summary

Capitalization	12
Language Usage	4
Punctuation:	
Comma	1
Hyphen	1
Period	2
Spelling	2

The butterfly unfolds its ~~delacut~~ (delicate) wings as it emerges
from the shell, blood pumps into the wings. After a few
hours, the butterfly can flap its wings ~~good~~ (well) enough to fly
away. This ~~inducates~~ (indicates) the beginning of the Adult stage.

four generations of monarchs are born each year.
butterflies from the first generation ~~is~~ (are) born in march and
april. Those from the second ~~is~~ (are) born in may and june.
Third-generation monarchs are born in july and august. All
of these butterflies live two to six weeks. Fourth-generation
butterflies, born in september and october, migrate south
and ~~lives~~ (live) for six to nine months.

Name _____

WEDNESDAY   Week 30

- apostrophes
- commas
- parentheses

After two weeks each plump caterpillar is approximately two inchs long, and fully grown. It stops eating and then spins a sticky, silk thred which it uses to fastens it self, hanging inverted, to a stem or a leaf. It shed it's skin of black white and yellow stripes and becomes a chrysalis (also called a pupa. This is the next stage of the monarchs life cycle. The shell around the Pupa grajally hardens and becomes opaque. Inside the shell, the body of the former caterpillar transforms into a butterfly. From the out side, it look as if nothing is taking place, the metamorphosis (which means a "change in form" occurs in less than two weeks.

THURSDAY   Week 30

- run-on sentences
- adverbs
- months

The butterfly unfolds its delacut wings as it emerges from the shell, blood pumps into the wings. After a few hours the butterfly can flap its wings good enough to fly away. This inducates the beginning of the Adult stage.

tour generations of monarchs are born each year butterflies from the first generation is born in march and april. Those from the second is born in may and june. Third-generation monarchs are born in july and august. All of these butterflies live two to six weeks. Fourth generation butterflies, born in september and october, migrate south and lives for six to nine months.

MONDAY   Week 31

The Fox and the Goat

One day, a fox fell by acident [accident] into a deap [deep] well. He looked around for a means of escape, but couldn't find none [one]. The rope for lowering buckets, and hoisting them up again, was at the top of the well, so he had no rope to hall [haul] himself up with. He also couldn't find no [any] footholds for climbing up. The fox treaded water until he was exausted [exhausted]; he knew that the end was near unless someone rescued him soon. Presintly [Presently], the fox heard jostling noises at the top of the well. A goat was piering [peering] over the ledge to see if there was any water in the well, and he cawt [caught] sight of the fox.

Error Summary

Capitalization	3
Language Usage	2
Punctuation:	
Apostrophe	1
Comma	5
Period	1
Spelling	7

TUESDAY   Week 31

"Hello, mr. [Mr.] Fox," he called down. "Is the water fresh or stagnant?"

The fox adopted a mery [merry] attitude to mask his destress [distress]. Trying to entice the goat, the fox responded that "the water was too excellant [excellent] to describe. Come on down and see for yourself," said the sly fox.

Indeed, the goat was exceedingly thristy [thirsty]. He had thought of nothing but his thirst for the past hour, and he was elated at having found the well. Without thinking twice about it, the goat plunged into the well. As soon as he did, the fox pointed out the predicament that both of them were in now.

Error Summary

Capitalization	2
Punctuation:	
Comma	6
Quotation Mark	5
Spelling	4

Name _____

The Fox and the Goat

One day, a Fox fell by acident into a deap well. He looked around for a means of escape, but couldnt find none. The rope for lowering buckets, and hoisting them up again, was at the top of the well so he had no rope to hall himself up with. He also couldn't find no footholds for climbing up. The fox treaded water until he was exausted, he knew that the end was near unless someone rescued him soon. Presintly, the fox heard jostling noises at the top of the well. A Goat was piering over the ledge to see if there was any water in the well and he cawt sight of the fox.

- commas
- run-on sentences
- double negatives

"Hello, mr. Fox" he called down. Is the water fresh or stagnant"?

The fox adopted a mery attitude to mask his destress. Trying to entice the goat, the fox responded that "the water was too excellant to describe." Come on down and see for yourself said the sly fox.

Indeed the Goat was exceedingly thristy. He had thought of nothing but his thirst for the past hour and he was elated at having found the well. Without thinking twice about it the goat plunged into the well. As soon as he did the fox pointed out the predicament that both of them were in now.

- personal names
- dialogue
- commas

WEDNESDAY   Week 31

"~~Do'nt~~ Don't worry, though, said the fox. "I have ~~a~~ an idea for a way that we both can get out of this mess. If you place your front hoofs on the wall and ~~bent~~ bend your head, I will climb onto your back and jump out of the well. Then, when I am rested, I will help you get out."

The goat ~~agrees~~ agreed. After all, what was the alternative? So he steadied himself by leaning against the wall, with his front hoofs. The fox quickly scrambled up the goat's back and ~~leeped~~ leaped to the top of the well. He cleared the ledge and ~~keeps~~ kept running without even glancing back. Before he got ~~to~~ too far, he heard the goat calling to him.

hoofs + hooves are both ok

Error Summary

Language Usage	4
Punctuation:	
Apostrophe	1
Comma	2
Period	1
Question Mark	1
Quotation Mark	3
Spelling	3

THURSDAY   Week 31

The fox ~~hezetated~~ hesitated, but returned to the well. He looked down at the struggling goat, who bleated up to him, "What are you doing? You promised to help me get out of here! Why are you breaking ~~you're~~ your promise!"

"What a fool you are! exclaimed the fox to the helpless goat. "What did you think would happen when you jumped into the well? You shouldn't have jumped before ~~haveing~~ having a plan to get out. How could you expose yourself to dangers that you were unprepared to face? And with that query, the uncaring fox slipped away. And the ~~morale~~ moral of the story is: Look before you ~~leaps~~ leap.

Error Summary

Language Usage	1
Punctuation:	
Comma	3
Exclamation Point	1
Question Mark	4
Quotation Mark	4
Spelling	4

Name _____

WEDNESDAY   Week 31

"Do'nt worry, though, said the fox. I have a idea for a way that we both can get out of this mess. If you place your front hoofs on the wall and bent your head. I will climb onto your back and jump out of the well. Then, when I am rested, I will help you get out.

The goat agrees. After all, what was the alternative. So he steadied himself by leaning against the wall, with his front hoofs. The fox quickly scrambled up the goats back and leeped to the top of the well. He cleared the ledge and keeps running without even glancing back. Before he got to far, he heard the goat calling to him?

- dialogue
- incomplete sentences
- end punctuation

THURSDAY   Week 31

The fox hezetated, but returned to the well. He looked down at the struggling goat, who bleated up to him "What are you doing. You promised to help me get out of here! Why are you breaking you're promise!

"What a fool you are exclaimed the fox to the helpless goat. What did you think would happen when you jumped into the well. You shouldn't have jumped before haveing a plan to get out. How could you expose yourself to dangers that you were unprepared to face And with that query the uncaring fox slipped away. And the morale or the story is: Look before you leaps.

- verbs
- dialogue
- end punctuation

MONDAY   Week 32

Who Was Aesop?

Most people have heard of aesop, the ancient greek
storyteller. This ~~legendery~~ (legendary) author is ~~creditted~~ (credited) with hundreds
of fables, such as "The Lion and the mouse" and "the Fox
and the Goat. Like other ~~fabuls~~ (fables), Aesop's stories typically
feature animals, That ~~has~~ (have) human characteristics, and each
story leads to a moral, or lesson, about how to live. The
stories that Aesop created are familiar to us 2,500 years
later. But what do we know of the story teller himself? We
know ~~surprising~~ (surprisingly) little. There is no ~~substanshial~~ (substantial) evidence, in
fact, that Aesop even really existed.

Error Summary

Capitalization	7
Language Usage	2
Punctuation:	
Comma	4
Period	1
Question Mark	1
Quotation Mark	1
Spelling	5

TUESDAY   Week 32

Several Ancient sources ~~write~~ (wrote) about Aesop as if he
were a real person. The ancient Greek ~~filosopher~~ (philosopher) aristotle
~~claim~~ (claimed) that Aesop was born around 620 B.C. near the black
sea. (Aristotle himself was born about 300 year's later,
so he was not alive during Aesops time) The ancient Greek
historian herodotus, who lived during the fifth century BC
~~report~~ (reported) that Aesop had been a slave who resided in the
Greek city-state of samos. Aesop's first master was Xanthus,
his second master was Iadmon, who ~~eventualy~~ (eventually) gave Aesop his
freedom. Aesop died around 560 b.c. in delphi where he had
~~went~~ (gone) as a ~~royel~~ (royal) ~~delegit~~ (delegate).

Error Summary

Capitalization	11
Language Usage	4
Punctuation:	
Apostrophe	2
Comma	3
Period	3
Semicolon	1
Spelling	4

Name _____

MONDAY   Week 32

Who Was Aesop?

Most people have heard of aesop, Storyteller. This legendery author is cr[...] of fables, such as "The Lion and The [...] and the Goat. Like other fabuls, Aeso[...] feature animals. That has human characteristics and each story leads to a moral or lesson, about how to live. The stories that Aesop created are familiar to us 2,500 years later. But what do we know of the story teller himself. We know surprising little. There is no substanshial evidence in fact that. Aesop even really existed.

- personal names
- story titles
- compound words
- adverbs

TUESDAY   Week 32

Several Ancient sources write about Aesop as if he were a real person. The ancient Greek filosopher aristotle claim that Aesop was born around 620 B.C. near the black sea. (Aristotle himself was born about 300 year's later so he was not alive during Aesops time). The ancient Greek historian herodotus, who lived during the Fifth Century BC report that Aesop had been a slave who resided in the Greek city-state of samos. Aesop's first master was Xanthus, his second master was Iadmon, who eventualy gave Aesop his freedom. Aesop died around 560 b.c. in delphi where he had went as a royel delegit.

- personal names
- place names
- abbreviations
- semicolons

WEDNESDAY   Week 32

Error Summary

Language Usage	4
Punctuation:	
Comma	4
Period	1
Question Mark	1
Spelling	8

These ~~biographicle~~ **biographical** details about ~~Easop~~ **Aesop** might be true⊙ On the other hand, Aristotle and Herodotus might have just repeated information that ~~come~~ **came** from popular stories ~~past~~ **passed** down through the years. It was a very, long time ago, and it is difficult to ~~verrafy~~ **verify** ancient sources. Modern ~~historiuns~~ **historians** have not been able to find any official ~~reckerds~~ **records** to prove that Aesop existed. Moreover, even if Aesop had been a real person, there is no evidence that he wrote any of the hundreds of ~~fabels~~ **fables** that made him famous. No one has ~~never~~ **ever** discovered stories ~~wrote~~ **written** in Aesop's own hand or ~~sined~~ **signed** by him. So where did Aesop's fables ~~came~~ **come** from,**?**

THURSDAY   Week 32

Error Summary

Capitalization	10
Language Usage	3
Punctuation:	
Comma	3
Hyphen	1
Period	3
Spelling	3

Many writers from ancient times mentioned Aesop's fables⊙ In their own writing. Mostly they ~~refered~~ **referred** to Aesop as a storyteller. **T**he stories ~~theirselves~~ **themselves** are probably traditional; they may even ~~had~~ **have** come from Persia, India, or other places. The first known collection of Aesop's fables appeared in the fourth-century BC. They were compiled by a Greek statesman named **D**emetrius⊙ but the collection ~~were~~ **was** lost during the **M**iddle **A**ges. The **R**oman writer Phaedrus translated the stories into **L**atin during the first century **B.C.** His versions express wit and ~~wisdam~~ **wisdom** **A**nd are ~~apreeshiated~~ **appreciated** to this day. They have been translated into many other languages.

Name _____

WEDNESDAY   Week 32

WATCH FOR

- verbs
- commas
- double negatives
- end punctuation

These biographicle details about Easop might be true On the other hand Aristotle and Herodotus might have just repeated information that come from popular stories past down through the years. It was a very, long time ago, and it is difficult to verrafy ancient sources. Modern historiuns have not been able to find any official reckerds to prove that Aesop existed. Moreover even if Aesop had been a real person there is no evidence that he wrote any of the hundreds of fabels that made him famous. No one has never discovered stories wrote in Aesop's own hand or sined by him. So where did Aesop's fables came from.

THURSDAY   Week 32

WATCH FOR

- incomplete sentences
- periods in history
- hyphens

Many writers from ancient times mentioned Aesop's fables. In their own writing. Mostly they refered to Aesop as a storyteller. the stories theirselves are probably traditional; they may even had come from Persia India or other places. The first known collection of Aesop's fables appeared in the fourth-century BC. They were compiled by a Greek statesman named demetrius but the collection were lost during the middle ages. The roman writer Phaedrus translated the stories into latin during the first century b.c. His versions express wit and wisdam. And are apreeshiated to this day. They have been translated into many other languages.

MONDAY   Week 33

Error Summary

Capitalization	2
Language Usage	3
Punctuation:	
Bracket	1
Comma	1
Ellipses	1
Parentheses	2
Underlined Words	4
Spelling	5

Tortoises Bounce Back

When Charles darwin sailed to the Galápagos Islands
(an archipelago [island cluster] near ecuador) in 1835, he
noticed
notices that each island had a distinctly different species
observation
of giant tortoises. It was this observasion, in part, that
led   theory
leads him to develop his thiery of evolution through natural
selection   are
sellection. Today, all species of giant Galápagos tortoises is
endangered. Sadly, one species (Chelonoidis elephantopus, or
extinct
C. elephantopus) was already extint as early as 1850 . . or so
people thought. Recently, though, scientists discovered that
after all
this species may not be extinct afterall.

TUESDAY   Week 33

Error Summary

Capitalization	3
Language Usage	4
Punctuation:	
Apostrophe	3
Comma	2
Spelling	7

The giant tortoises of the galápagos islands are some
largest   reptiles
of the most large reptiels that still roam the planet. Adults
weigh
of some species way more than 600 pounds, and exceed five
feet in length. Long ago, the crews' of whaling ships hunted
source   stored
these animals as a sorce of food and oil. They storred the
or
live tortoises in a ships' hull for months with out food nor
water; they cruelly placed the animals on their backs to
escaping
prevent them from escape. People brought other threats to
tortoises   consumed
the tortises. Rats from ships consoomed the tortoise egg's
which caused tortoise populations to decline. Goats and Pigs
vegetation   eaten
ate the vegetation that tortoises would have ate.

MONDAY   Week 33

Tortoises Bounce Back

When Charles darwin sailed to the Galápagos Islands
(an archipelago [island cluster) near ecuador] in 1835, he
notices that each island had a distinctly different species
of giant tortoises. It was this observasion, in part, that
leads him to develop his thiery of evolution through natural
sellection. Today, all species of giant Galápagos tortoises is
endangered. Sadly, one species (Chelonoidis elephantopus, or
C. elephantopus was already extint as early as 1850 .. or so
people thought. Recently though, scientists discovered that
this species may not be extinct afterall.

WATCH FOR
- parentheses
- brackets
- scientific names
- ellipses

TUESDAY   Week 33

The giant tortoises of the galápagos islands are some
of the most large reptiels that still roam the planet. Adults
of some species way more than 600 pounds, and exceed five
feet in length. Long ago, the crews' of whaling ships hunted
these animals as a sorce of food and oil. They storred the
live tortoises in a ships' hull for months with out food nor
water; they cruelly placed the animals on their backs to
prevent them from escape. People brought other threats to
the tortises. Rats from ships consoomed the tortoise egg's
which caused tortoise populations to decline. Goats and Pigs
ate the vegatation that tortoises would have ate.

WATCH FOR
- place names
- apostrophes
- verbs
- double negatives

WEDNESDAY   Week 33

An
A article in the journal <u>Current Biology</u>, published in

january 2012, announced a scientific study of 1,669 tortoises

living on isabela island, one of the islands in the Archipelago.

Biologists took blood samples and compared the genetic code

of these tortoises against a genetic database of all tortoise

quite
species. The results were quiet surprising. Eighty-four of

the tortoises studied have one parent that is entirely of

the <u>C. elephantopus</u> species. Some of those parents may still

alive
be allive today, given that tortoises can live for more than

a
100 years. If scientists find them, they can start an breeding

program to revive the species.

Error Summary

Capitalization	4
Language Usage	2
Punctuation:	
Comma	2
Hyphen	1
Underlined Words	4
Spelling	2

THURSDAY   Week 33

perplexed
Researchers are purplexed about how the Tortoises

turned up on Isabela island in the first place. During darwins

time, the C. Elephantopus tortoises were living on one of

the Southernmost islands of the archipelago. Isabela is on

Researchers
the northwestern edge of the archipelago. Reserchers now

speculate
speculates that the tortoises had been stowed aboard whaling

ships or Pirate ships and dumped at sea to lighten the load

in the ships' hulls. The tortoise's cannot swim, but they float

well
good. They may have floated on the ocean currents and

bred
landed on Isabela, where they breeded with tortoises native

to that island. In any case, the species apparently survived.

Error Summary

Capitalization	6
Language Usage	3
Punctuation:	
Apostrophe	3
Period	2
Spelling	2

Name _____

WEDNESDAY   Week 33

- magazine titles
- hyphens
- scientific names

A article in the journal Current Biology, published in january 2012, announced a scientific study of 1,669 tortoises living on isabela island, one of the islands in the Archipelago. Biologists took blood samples and compared the genetic code of these tortoises against a genetic database of all tortoise species. The results were quiet surprising. Eighty four of the tortoises studied have one parent that is entirely of the C. elephantopus species. Some of those parents may still be allive today given that tortoises can live for more than 100 years. If scientists find them they can start an breeding program to revive the species.

THURSDAY   Week 33

- apostrophes
- scientific names

Researchers are purplexed about how the Tortoises turned up on Isabela island in the first place? During darwins time, the C Elephantopus tortoises were living on one of the Southernmost islands of the archipelago. Isabela is on the northwestern edge of the archipelago. Reserchers now speculates that the tortoises had been stowed aboard whaling ships or Pirate ships and dumped at sea to lighten the load in the ships hulls. The tortoise's cannot swim, but they float good. They may have floated on the ocean currents and landed on Isabela, where they breeded with tortoises native to that island. In any case, the species apparently survived.

MONDAY   Week 34

The Taj Mahal

Many people consider the Taj Mahal to be the ~~more~~ [most]
beautiful building in the world. The structure is located in
agra, a small city in Northern india. Built by the Mughal
emperor shah jahan, the [Taj Mahal] ~~purpose~~ was [meant] to honor his wife and
to memorialize her. The building's name is derived from the
name of the emperor's wife, mumtaz mahal (which means
"chosen one of the palace") Her death in 1631 ended a
[marriage] ~~mariage~~ of nineteen years. Her grief-stricken husband ~~begun~~ [began]
building the structure the following year. Construction and
decoration ~~continue~~ [continued] for twenty-two years.

Error Summary

Capitalization	7
Language Usage	3
Punctuation:	
Apostrophe	2
Hyphen	2
Parentheses	1
Sentence Structure	1
Spelling	1

TUESDAY   Week 34

The Taj Mahal has five main parts: The main gateway,
the garden, the mosque, the jawab (a building that mirrors
the mosque), and the mausoleum (which has four minarets).
The design of all of the parts ~~are~~ [is] a blend of indian, persian,
and islamic architectural styles. the mausoleum itself is made
of cream-colored marble. The building ~~seem~~ [seems] to change colors
according to the ~~intencity~~ [intensity] of the sunlight. the marble walls
appear pink, yellow, or the color of apricots, depending on the
time of day or night. In the evening, ~~it appears~~ [they appear] warm brown.
Later, when the smooth walls reflect the moon light, they
take on a cool blue-gray cast.

Error Summary

Capitalization	6
Language Usage	4
Punctuation:	
Comma	7
Parentheses	1
Period	2
Spelling	2

Name _____

The Taj Mahal

Many people consider the Taj Mahal to be the more beautiful building in the world. The structure is located in agra, a small city in Northern india. Built by the Mughal emperor shah jahan, the purpose was to honor his wife and to memorialize her. The buildings name is derived from the name of the emperors wife, mumtaz mahal (which means "chosen one of the palace". Her death in 1631 ended a mariage of nineteen years. Her grief stricken husband begun building the structure the following year. Construction and decoration continue for twenty two years.

* parentheses
* dangling modifiers
* hyphens

The Taj Mahal has five main parts: The main gateway the garden the mosque the jawab (a building that mirrors the mosque, and the mausoleum (which has four minarets). The design of all of the parts are a blend of indian persian and islamic architectural styles. the mausoleum itself is made of cream-colored marble. The building seem to change colors according to the intencity of the sunlight. the marble walls appear pink yellow or the color of apricots, depending on the time of day or night In the evening, it appears warm brown. Later, when the smooth walls reflect the moon light, they take on a cool blue-gray cast

* parentheses
* cultural identities
* pronouns
* run-on sentences

WEDNESDAY　　　　　　　　　　Week 34

The mausoleums four walls are near identacle. Each *(nearly identical)* has *(has)* have a wide arch in the center that is 108 feet (33 meters) tall. The dome in the middle is 240 feet (73 meters) high. four smaller domes surround it. The dome shape has an effect *(effect)* affect on sound. If you was *(were)* to blow a single note on a flute, it wood *(would)* echo five time's. Inside the mausoleum is an eight-sided marble chamber decorated with carvings and semiprecious stones. This area also houses two cenotaphs also known as false tomb's surrounded by an intricately carved marble screen. Under the false tombs, at garden level, is *(are)* the real tombs of mumtaz mahal and shah jahan.

Error Summary

Capitalization	4
Language Usage	5
Punctuation:	
Apostrophe	4
Comma	3
Hyphen	1
Parentheses	2
Semicolon	1
Spelling	2

THURSDAY　　　　　　　　　　Week 34

Two identical buildings flank the mausoleum they are the mosque, which face *(faces)* east, and its jawab (mirror image) which faces west. These buildings are made mostly of Red Sandstone, providing a contrast in color and texture with the white marbel *(marble)* of the mausoleum. Walking paths, fountains and ornamental trees adorn the garden that surround *(surrounds)* the buildings. The central pools of the garden captures *(capture)* the reflection of the mausoleum Making a striking picture. Calligraphy and fancy geometric designs of inlaid stones decorates *(decorate)* the buildings. Its no wonder that more than three million people visit this architectural gem annually.

Error Summary

Capitalization	4
Language Usage	4
Punctuation:	
Apostrophe	1
Comma	3
Hyphen	1
Period	1
Spelling	1

Name _____

WEDNESDAY   Week 34

The mausoleums four wall's are near identacle. Each have a wide arch in the center that is 108 feet (33 meters tall. The dome in the middle is 240 feet 73 meters) high, four smaller domes surround it. The dome shape has an affect on sound. If you was to blow a single note on a flute, it wood echo five time's. Inside the mausoleum is an eight sided marble chamber decorated with carvings and semiprecious stones. This area also houses two cenotaphs also known as false tomb's surrounded by an intricately carved marble screen. Under the false tombs, at garden level, is the real tombs, of mumtaz mahal and shah jahan.

WATCH FOR
- apostrophes
- semicolons
- hyphens

THURSDAY   Week 34

Two identical buildings flank the mausoleum, they are the mosque, which face east, and its <u>jawab</u> (mirror image) which faces west. These buildings are made mostly of Red Sandstone, providing a contrast in color and texture with the white marbel of the mausoleum. Walking paths, fountains and ornamental trees adorn the garden that surround the buildings. The central pools of the garden captures the reflection of the mausoleum. Making a striking picture. Calligraphy and fancy geometric designs of inlaid stones decorates the buildings. Its no wonder that more than three-million people visit this architectural gem annually.

WATCH FOR
- commas
- incomplete sentences
- hyphens
- verbs

MONDAY   Week 35

Should P.E. Affect Your GPA?

Physical fitness is important to good health, and
offering physical education (P.E.) classes gives students the
chance to get in shape, stay in shape, compete in sports and
release energy each day. But how important is PE as a school
subject? Ultimately, the grades you receive in P.E. affect your
overall grade-point average (GPA). That isn't fair. Given that
P.E. isn't an academic subject. In my opinion, only subjects
such as Math Science History and English should count,
because those are the only ones that lead to academic
success. P.E. grades should not affect your gpa.

Error Summary

Capitalization	7
Language Usage	1
Punctuation:	
Comma	5
Hyphen	1
Parentheses	1
Period	2
Question Mark	1
Spelling	4

TUESDAY   Week 35

One reason that P.E. grades should not count is that
people have different physical capabilities. Some students
perform well in p.e. class, but others do not. What about
students who have health problems, such as asthma or
anemia? They may not be able to run as fast or as far as
healthier kids can. Supporters of the current grading
policy may argue that people have different academic
abilities, too. That's true, but aren't those the very skills
that should count toward academic achievement? Getting into
Advanced Placement (a.p.) classes or into a good college should
not depend on how well you do in P.E.

Error Summary

Capitalization	4
Language Usage	3
Punctuation:	
Apostrophe	2
Comma	3
Parentheses	2
Question Mark	2
Spelling	5

Name _____

Should P.E. Affect Your GPA?

Physical fitness is important to good health, and offerring physical education (P.E.) classes give students the chance to get in shape, stay in shape, compeat in sports and release energy each day. But how important is PE as a school subject. Ultimitely, the grades you receive in P.E. affect your overall grade point average (GPA. That isn't fair. Given that P.E. isn't an academic subject. In my opinion, only subjects such as Math Science History and English should count, because those are the only ones that lead to accademic success. P.E. grades should not affect your gpa.

- abbreviations
- verbs
- hyphens
- end punctuation

One reason that P.E. grades should not count, is that people have different physical capabilties. Some students perform good in p.e. class, but others do not. What about students who have health problems, such as asthma or anemia. They may not be able to run as fast, nor as far as more healthy kids can. Supportors of the current gradeing policy may argue, that people have different acaddemic abilities, too. Thats true, but arent those the very skills that should count toward academic acheivement. Getting into Advanced Placement a.p. classes or into a good college should not depend on how well you do in P.E.

- abbreviations
- words that compare
- double negatives
- end punctuation

WEDNESDAY   Week 35

Another reason that P.E. grades should not count is that it's better for schools to ~~encouridge~~ *encourage* kids to enjoy physical education instead of making kids do sports for a grade. Students should not feel ~~stresed~~ *stressed* out about doing ~~good~~ *well* in p.e. If they enjoy it, that's great; if they're good athletes, that's fine. But they shouldn't feel pressured to be ~~atheletic~~ *athletic* just for a grade. Furthermore, they shouldn't be forced to be ~~compettitive~~ *competitive*. Many of the sports that schools teach in P.E. are games in which there is a winner, and a ~~losser~~ *loser*. In a math or english class, for example, every one can get ~~a~~ *an* a; there are no winners ~~nor~~ *or* losers.

Error Summary

Capitalization	5
Language Usage	3
Punctuation:	
Apostrophe	3
Comma	4
Period	2
Semicolon	1
Spelling	6

THURSDAY   Week 35

Now, I'm not ~~sugesting~~ *suggesting* that schools ~~elimenate~~ *eliminate* P.E. classes. And I don't object to P.E. teachers giving letter grades to students; some students, in fact, perform better if they are graded. However, I strongly believe that P.E. grades should not count toward a student's overall GPA unless that student specifically ~~request~~ *requests* it. (A student ~~that~~ *who* ~~exels~~ *excels* in sports may depend on the A that ~~him~~ *he* or ~~her~~ *she* gets in a P.E. class to boost ~~a~~ *an* overall GPA. In that case, the school may count the P.E. grade.) It is my recommendation that all schools ~~adopts~~ *adopt* a new policy: Including P.E. grades in the GPA should be optional, and students can decide for ~~theirselves~~ *themselves*.

Error Summary

Language Usage	7
Punctuation:	
Apostrophe	2
Comma	4
Semicolon	1
Spelling	3

Name _____

WEDNESDAY	Week 35

Another reason that P.E. grades should not count is that its better for schools to encouridge kids to enjoy physical education instead of making kids do sports for a grade. Students should not feel stresed out about doing good in p.e. If they enjoy it, thats great, if they're good athletes, that's fine. But they shouldn't feel pressured to be atheletic just for a grade. Furthermore they shouldnt be forced to be compettitive. Many of the sports that schools teach in P.E are games in which there is a winner, and a losser. In a math or english class for example every one can get a a, there are no winners nor losers.

- abbreviations
- semicolons
- words that compare
- double negatives

THURSDAY	Week 35

Now I'm not sugesting that schools elimenate P.E. classes. And I dont object to P.E. teachers giving letter grades to students, some students in fact perform better if they are graded. However I strongly believe that P.E. grades should not count toward a students overall GPA unless that student specifically request it. (A student that exels in sports may depend on the A that him or her gets in a P.E. class to boost a overall GPA. In that case, the school may count the P.E. grade.) It is my recommendation that all schools adopts a new policy: Including P.E. grades in the GPA should be optional, and students can decide for theirselves.

- semicolons
- commas
- pronouns

MONDAY   Week 36

Bud, Not Buddy

The novel <u>Bud</u>, <u>Not</u> <u>Buddy</u> is about an ten-year-old
motherless boy who sets out to find his father. The story,
written by christopher paul curtis takes place in michigan in
1936. the story's protagonist is the young boy bud caldwell
who has lived in a Orphanage since the age of six. The
novel follows Buds adventures as he travels from Flint to
grand rapids Michigan. Bud is also the narrator, and his
voice is that of a good-natured kid who is self-reliant and
determined. His voice provides many funny, and honnest
moments in this sometimes dark story.

Error Summary

Capitalization	10
Language Usage	2
Punctuation:	
Apostrophe	3
Comma	5
Hyphen	4
Underlined Words	3
Spelling	2

TUESDAY   Week 36

Bud runs away from an harsh foster home, taking his
suit case full of personal mementos. The treasures include
flyers that avvertise different jazz bands led by a musician
named herman e calloway. Bud has reason to beleive that
Calloway is his father (although hes wrong. the city mentioned
on one of the flyers give Bud a destinashun for his search.
on his journey, Bud meets many people whom help him.
A family waiting in line at the mission pretends that Bud
belongs to them their kindness prevent Bud from going
hungry that day. Another character, lefty lewis, gives Bud
a ride and asists him in finding Calloway.

Error Summary

Capitalization	8
Language Usage	4
Punctuation:	
Apostrophe	1
Parentheses	1
Period	2
Spelling	5

Name _____

Bud, Not Buddy

The novel Bud, Not Buddy is about an ten year old motherless boy who sets out to find his father. The story, written by christopher paul curtis takes place in michigan in 1936. the storys protagonist is the young boy bud caldwell who has lived in a Orphanage since the age of six. The novel follows Buds adventure's as he travels from Flint to grand rapids Michigan. Bud is also the narrater, and his voice is that of a good natured kid who is self reliant and determined. His voice provides many funny, and honnest moments in this sometimes dark story.

- book titles
- commas
- hyphens
- place names

Bud runs away from an harsh foster home, taking his suit case full of personal mementos. The treasures include flyers that avvertise different jazz bands led by a musician named herman e calloway. Bud has reason to beleive that Calloway is his father (although hes wrong. the city mentioned on one of the flyers give Bud a destinashun for his search. on his journey, Bud meets many people whom help him. A family waiting in line at the mission pretends that Bud belongs to them, their kindness prevent Bud from going hungry that day. Another character, lefty lewis, gives Bud a ride and asists him in finding Calloway.

- personal names
- compound words

WEDNESDAY — Week 36

Bud̂s "rules for ~~survivul~~ survival" are funny, but also ~~perseptive~~ perceptive. Rule number 3 says: "If you have to tell a lie, make sure it̂s simple and easy to remember." Bud figures out many things on his own, but he also recalls lessons that his mother taught him before she died. She used to say, "When one door closes, don̂t worry, because another door opens." Her statement ~~express~~ expresses one of the book̂s ~~centrel~~ central themes, Which many events ~~shows~~ show. For example, Bud discovers that the ~~librarean~~ librarian he was depending on has moved away. Just then, as hês wondering what to do next, a friend from the orphanage arrives. The two boys ~~than~~ then travel together for a while.

Error Summary

Capitalization	1
Language Usage	3
Punctuation:	
Apostrophe	5
Comma	5
Quotation Mark	3
Spelling	4

THURSDAY — Week 36

Reading <u>Bud</u>, <u>Not</u> <u>Buddy</u> is ~~a exelent~~ an excellent way to learn about life during the depression. It was a time when millions of people ~~was~~ were unemployed, thousands of homeless people lived in makeshift towns called Hoovervilles. The towns were named for president Herbert hoover, many people thought Hoover was ~~responsable~~ responsible for letting the ~~econnemy~~ economy fail.

When bud stays in the Hooverville outside of Flint, he learns about riding the rails, that was how many people went around looking for work in the 1930s. Bud tries to ride the rails but isn̂t fast enough. Missing the train turns out to be lucky, though. He finds Calloway and his search is over.

Error Summary

Capitalization	7
Language Usage	2
Punctuation:	
Apostrophe	1
Period	3
Underlined Words	3
Spelling	3

Name _____

WEDNESDAY   Week 36

Buds "rules for survivul" are funny, but also perseptive. Rule number 3 says: "If you have to tell a lie, make sure its simple and easy to remember. Bud figures out many things on his own but he also recalls lessons that his mother taught him before she died. She used to say, When one door closes, dont worry, because another door opens. Her statement express one of the books centrel themes. Which many events shows. For example Bud discovers that the librarean he was depending on has moved away. Just then, as hes wondering what to do next a friend from the orphanage arrives. The two boys than travel together for a while.

- run-on sentences
- quotations
- apostrophes

THURSDAY   Week 36

Reading Bud, Not Buddy is a exelent way to learn about life during the depression. It was a time when millions of people was unemployed, thousands of homeless people lived in makeshift towns called Hoovervilles. The towns were named for president Herbert hoover, many people thought Hoover was responsable for letting the econnemy fail.

When bud stays in the Hooverville outside of Flint, he learns about riding the rails, that was how many people went around looking for work in the 1930s. Bud tries to ride the rails but isnt fast enough. Missing the train turns out to be lucky, though. He finds Calloway and his search is over.

- book titles
- periods in history
- personal names

Write a short essay to compare two other activities that are similar in some ways but different in other ways. For example, you might compare and contrast sumo wrestling and freestyle wrestling, tennis and table tennis, baseball and softball, or drawing and painting. Choose activities that you are somewhat familiar with. In your introductory paragraph, mention the two activities that you are comparing. In subsequent paragraphs, give details about the activities. Be sure to tell at least one way in which the activities are similar and one way they are different.

Think of a skill, such as using chopsticks, that you know well and could teach others how to do. Write a brief how-to article to share your knowledge. Be sure to order the steps sequentially and use precise language that makes the process clear. Consider one of the following topics, or choose one of your own:

- How to set the table

- How to play the harmonica

- How to play Sudoku

Write one or two paragraphs about the experience that immigrants had as they passed through Ellis Island. Begin with one of the following sentences, or write your own:

- More than twenty million people left Europe and came to the United States between 1870 and 1910.

- Ellis Island was the first impression that most immigrants had of the United States at the turn of the twentieth century.

- The Ellis Island experience was probably a frightening one for many people entering the United States for the first time.

Write one or two paragraphs about the myth of Echo and Narcissus. Begin with one of the following sentences, or write your own:

- Have you ever wondered how the ancient Greeks explained the scientific phenomenon of the echo?

- The myth about Echo and Narcissus is one of the saddest in Greek mythology.

- Echo thought she was clever, but she couldn't fool Hera forever.

In one or two paragraphs, explain what you have learned about honeybees. Begin with one of the following sentences, or write your own:

- The life of a honeybee is truly amazing.

- Although honeybees may look the same, they are not created equal.

- Honeybees are smarter than you might think.

Write one or two paragraphs about the fictional O'Donnell family. You may want to continue the story or tell what happened before they decided to leave Ireland. Include historical details about the Irish famine in the 1840s, the journey across the Atlantic Ocean, or starting a new life in Boston. Begin with one of the following sentences, or write your own:

- Danny trembled with excitement as he walked the dusty streets of Boston.

- Patrick and Fiona O'Donnell had some serious thinking to do.

Using the same voice as the narrator in "The King's Cupcakes," write one or two paragraphs that elaborate on or provide more background for one of the scenes in the story. Begin with one of the following sentences, or write your own:

- "Let me bake an apple pie for you," said Queen Appelonia, "and you will see what I mean."

- Because Queen Malicious was not as good as she was beautiful, no one in her kingdom tried to save her from the dragon.

- Queen Plain Jane was furious.

Write one or two paragraphs describing a vivarium you have seen before or one that you would like to put together. Begin with one of the following sentences, or write your own:

- A desert vivarium is easy to maintain.

- A vivarium with frogs and salamanders can be very colorful and interesting.

- If you mix desert plants and water-loving animals in a vivarium, the results can be a disaster.

Write the beginning of a story that shows how characters deal with an ethical dilemma similar to the one described in "Student Elections." Use the following story starters for ideas:

- Janice was shocked to see how the bully treated the new kid.

- Pedro saw Angelo cheat by copying from Alice's test paper, and he wasn't sure what to do about it.

- Jerome knew who was spraying graffiti on the garage doors in his neighborhood.

FRIDAY – WEEK 10   **History Article: Triangle Shirtwaist Factory Fire**

Write one or two paragraphs about the fire at the Triangle Shirtwaist Factory. You may want to focus on the working conditions inside the factory. Begin with one of the following sentences, or write your own:

- The fire at the Triangle Shirtwaist Factory was a terrible tragedy.

- Could the fire at the Triangle Shirtwaist Factory have been prevented?

FRIDAY – WEEK 11   **Short Story: The Snake Charmer**

Briefly retell the story "The Snake Charmer" from the point of view of Daniel. Begin with one of the following sentences, or write your own:

- Daniel was quite startled when India wrapped herself around his waist.

- "If she squeezes much tighter, I'll probably pass out," thought Daniel.

- Daniel had no idea a python could be so strong.

FRIDAY – WEEK 12   **Geography Article: A Sea That's Not a Sea**

Write one or two paragraphs about the Dead Sea. Begin with one of the following sentences, or write your own:

- The Dead Sea is unlike any other lake in the world.

- If you tried to swim underwater in the Dead Sea, you would find it impossible.

- A fisherman would have a very disappointing day on the Dead Sea.

In one or two paragraphs, describe the contributions that Georges Méliès made to film technology. Begin with one of the following sentences, or write your own:

- Have you ever wondered how film technology developed?

- The history of moving pictures goes back to the 1890s, when Georges Méliès was a young man.

- If you enjoy films, you owe a debt of gratitude to Georges Méliès.

Imagine that you are going to enter a science fair. Write one or two diary entries describing your project or experiment and any difficulties you might encounter. Begin with one of the following sentences, or write your own:

- The science fair is next week, and I still don't have an idea for a project.

- For the science fair, I think I'll demonstrate what happens to plants that are exposed to loud music.

- My project for last year's science fair was a disappointment, so this year I really want to do something exciting.

Write one or two paragraphs about the crash between the <u>Andrea</u> <u>Doria</u> and the <u>Stockholm</u>. Begin with one of the following sentences, or write your own:

- July 25, 1956, was a tragic day for the passengers and crew of the <u>Andrea</u> <u>Doria</u>.

- A terrible accident took place in the Atlantic Ocean in the summer of 1956.

- Not even radar could prevent a tragic accident caused by human error.

Write one or two paragraphs for a science article about spiders. Begin with one of the following sentences, or write your own:

- Scientists studying spiders have uncovered some amazing facts about these little creatures.

- Spiders are remarkable creatures.

- Even Little Miss Muffet would be fascinated by these facts about spiders.

Write one or two paragraphs about the life and exploits of Alain Robert. Begin with one of the following sentences, or write your own:

- Alain Robert climbs skyscrapers for the thrill of it—without a safety net.

- What would you do if you were locked out of your apartment?

- Alain Robert leads a dangerous life.

Write one or two paragraphs about how Susan B. Anthony and Elizabeth Cady Stanton helped secure voting rights for women in the United States. Begin with one of the following sentences, or write your own:

- Did you know that at one time women were not allowed to vote in the United States?

- Susan B. Anthony and Elizabeth Cady Stanton were brave women who stood up for their beliefs.

- In the fight for women's right to vote, Susan B. Anthony and Elizabeth Cady Stanton were fearless leaders.

"Four Days Without a Cellphone" is an anecdote—a short, amusing story about something that really happened. Write an anecdote about an incident in your life. Begin with one of the following sentences, or choose a topic of your own:

- The first time I went ice-skating, I thought it would be easy.

- When I first learned how to cook my own breakfast, it made me feel self-sufficient.

- I know how to wash laundry now, but I made mistakes in the beginning.

In one or two paragraphs, describe the characteristics and life cycle of the flamingo. Begin with one of the following sentences, or write your own:

- Have you ever observed flamingos at a zoo or in the wild?

- The flamingo is an unusual bird.

- Flamingos like to gather in huge flocks.

Write a one- or two-paragraph letter about a trip that you have taken or would like to take. Include the date, an appropriate salutation that ends with a comma, at least one body paragraph, an appropriate closing (also ending with a comma), and your signature.

In one or two paragraphs, explain why the harbor porpoises left San Francisco Bay and why they are now returning. Begin with one of the following sentences, or write your own:

- Environmentalists report that the harbor porpoises have returned to San Francisco Bay.

- It has been more than sixty years since they left, but the harbor porpoises are now coming back to the Bay Area.

- The return of the "puffing pigs" has Bay Area tourists and residents excited.

In one or two paragraphs, discuss the life of Billy Fisher. Begin with one of the following sentences, or write your own:

- When Billy Fisher was a young man, he became a rider for the Pony Express.

- The Pony Express hired many brave young men, Billy Fisher among them.

- The life of a Pony Express rider was full of peril, as Billy Fisher certainly could have told you.

In one or two paragraphs, tell why Balto is honored and remembered. Begin with one of the following sentences, or write your own:

- Nome, Alaska, was in need of lifesaving diphtheria antitoxin, but airplanes couldn't deliver it.

- Balto will always be remembered as the lead sled dog that reached Nome, Alaska, with needed serum in 1925.

- Balto was a brave, strong, and intelligent dog.

Write one or two paragraphs describing Liam's experience with his online order.
Begin with one of the following sentences, or write your own:

- Liam was very excited at the prospect of getting a rock from Saturn.

- Liam looked forward to sharing his amazing rock with his best friend, Adam.

- The idea of getting a rock from another planet had never occurred to Liam—
  until the day he read an online ad.

Write one or two paragraphs about the adventures of Pecos Bill. Include humor
and exaggeration, which are typical of tall tales. Begin with one of the following
sentences, or write your own:

- Pecos Bill never did things in small ways.

- Did you ever wonder how the Grand Canyon was formed?

- Death Valley wasn't always below sea level.

Joshua Wurman has always enjoyed building things. That pastime eventually led him
to his unusual profession. Write three interview questions to ask a partner about one
of his or her hobbies or pastimes that could lead to a profession or job later in life.
Then conduct an interview and present your questions to your partner. Record the
answers, and be sure to edit them.

Write one or two paragraphs to describe the project undertaken by the narrator and people in the neighborhood where Pettigrew Apartments used to be located. Begin with one of the following sentences, or write your own:

- The empty lot had become an eyesore.

- There had to be something that could be done about the trash- and weed-filled lot in the middle of the neighborhood.

- People can come together to make a difference in their communities.

In one or two paragraphs, explain what happens during sleep and why sleep is important to people's health. Begin with one of the following sentences, or write your own:

- Everyone needs sleep, but people have different sleep requirements.

- Sleep is good for the body as well as the mind.

- We spend about a third of our life sleeping.

Write one or two paragraphs about monarch butterflies. Begin with one of the following sentences, or write your own:

- The life cycle of a monarch butterfly is fascinating.

- For a monarch butterfly, September and October are the best months to be born.

- If you want to attract monarch butterflies to your yard, plant some milkweed.

In one or two paragraphs, write a fable that you are familiar with. Be sure to include the moral, or lesson, of the story. Or, if you prefer, write a new ending for "The Fox and the Goat." Think about another way in which the fox might react to hearing the goat calling from the well. How might the goat respond? Choose an ending that changes the moral of the story, and be sure to write the new moral.

In one or two paragraphs, describe who Aesop was. Begin with one of the following sentences, or write your own:

- Almost everyone knows at least one of Aesop's fables.

- Strangely enough, Aesop may be as fictitious as a fable.

- Most people think that Aesop was an ancient Greek writer.

Write one or two paragraphs that provide scientific facts about giant Galápagos tortoises. Or write the first one or two paragraphs of a science article about another endangered or threatened species. Describe the plant's or animal's appearance and habitat, and provide other details about the species, including why it is endangered or threatened.

The Taj Mahal is an impressive piece of architecture. In one or two paragraphs, describe a familiar building, bridge, tower, or other structure that you think is impressive. Focus on the appearance of the structure and the materials used in its construction. You may also want to include details about the history and purpose of the structure.

Write one or two paragraphs for a persuasive essay that argues the opposite viewpoint to that of "Should P.E. Affect Your GPA?" Begin with one of the following sentences, or write your own:

- Physical education is just as important as math, science, history, and English.

- Physical education teaches teamwork, self-discipline, and sportsmanship.

- For some students, physical education classes provide the only opportunity they'll ever have to experience different sports.

Write one or two paragraphs for a review of a book or story that you have read recently. State the title and author. Give a brief summary of the plot. Describe the characters, setting, and central themes. You may want to describe one or two key events, too. Include your opinion of the book or story, but support your statements with meaningful facts from the text, such as carefully chosen quotations. Include information that might prompt readers to seek that book—or to choose a different book instead.

Proofreading Marks

Use these marks to show corrections.

Mark	Meaning	Example
૬	Take this out (delete).	I love to ~~to~~ read.
⊙	Add a period.	It was late⊙
≡	Make this a capital letter.	First prize went to maria.
/	Make this a lowercase letter.	We saw a /Black /Cat.
——	Fix the spelling.	This is our ~~hause~~. (house)
˄	Add a comma.	Goodnight˄ Mom.
˅	Add an apostrophe.	It˅s mine.
˅˅ ˅˅	Add quotation marks.	Come in,˅ he said.
! ?	Add an exclamation point or a question mark.	Help! Can you help me?
˄	Add a hyphen.	Let's go in˄line skating after school.
‿	Close the space.	Foot‿ball is fun.
( ) [ ]	Add parentheses or brackets.	My favorite cereals (oatmeal [not instant] and granola) are healthful.
˄	Add a word or phrase.	The ˄pen is mine. (red)
——	Underline the words.	We read <u>Old</u> <u>Yeller</u>.
⨟ ⨟	Add a semicolon or a colon.	Alex arrived at 400 Mia arrived later.

Daily Paragraph Editing • EMC 2837 • © Evan-Moor Corp.

Language Handbook
Basic Rules for Writing and Editing

Contents

Capital Letters

Always use a **capital letter** to begin:

the first word of a sentence	Today is the first day of school.
the first word of a quotation, except when it continues the sentence	She said, "Today is the first day of school." **But:** "Today," she said, "is the first day of school."
the salutation (greeting) and the closing in a letter	Dear Grandma, Love, Sherry
the names of days, months, and holidays	The fourth Thursday in November is Thanksgiving.
people's first and last names, their initials, and their titles	Mrs. Cruz and her son Felix met with Principal Bill C. Lee. **Note:** Use abbreviations of titles (for example, Mr., Mrs., Dr., and Capt.) only when you also use the person's name. Did you see the **doctor** yesterday? Yes, I saw **Dr.** Carter.
a word that is used as part of a name or to replace someone's name	I went with Dad and Aunt Terry to visit Grandma. **But:** I went with my dad and my aunt to visit my grandma.
the names of nationalities and languages	Mexican, Cuban, and Nicaraguan people all speak Spanish.
the names of ethnic or cultural groups or geographic identities	There were Asian, Native American, and African dancers at the festival.
the names of ships, planes, and space vehicles	The president flew on Air Force One to see the USS Nimitz, a large U.S. Navy aircraft carrier. **Note:** You must also underline the name of the ship, plane, or space vehicle.
street names	Palm Avenue, Cypress Street, Pine Boulevard
cities, states, countries, and continents	Los Angeles, California, United States of America; Paris, France; Asia, Europe, South America
specific landforms and bodies of water	Great Plains, San Francisco Bay, the Great Lakes
buildings, monuments, and public places	the White House, the Statue of Liberty, Yellowstone National Park
historic events	The Gold Rush began in 1849. The Civil War ended in 1865.

Daily Paragraph Editing • EMC 2837 • © Evan-Moor Corp.

each word in the title of a book, story, poem, or magazine (except for a short, unimportant word such as *a, an, at, for, in,* and *the,* unless it is the first or last word of the title)	The story "The Friendly Fruit Bat" appeared in Ranger Rick magazine and in the science book Flying Mammals.
	
	Note: Underline some titles, but use quotation marks for others.
	    Book titles: Flowers for Algernon
	    Magazine titles: Ranger Rick
	    Movie titles: The Sound of Music
	    TV shows: The Simpsons
	    Newspapers: The Daily News
	But:
	    Story titles: "The Fox and the Crow"
	    Chapter titles: "In Which Piglet Meets a Heffalump"
	    Poem titles: "My Shadow"
	    Song titles: "Battle Hymn of the Republic"
	    Titles of articles: "Ship Sinks in Bay"

Punctuation Marks

Use a **period (.):**

to end a sentence that gives information	The Grand Canyon is in Arizona.
to end a sentence that gives a mild command	Choose a story to read aloud.
with abbreviations (days of the week, months, units of measure, time, etc.)	Jan. (January), Feb. (February), Mon. (Monday), ft. (foot or feet), oz. (ounce or ounces), 8:00 A.M.
with initials	Dr. A. J. Cronin

Use a **question mark (?)** to end a question:

- Did you choose a story to read?

Use an **exclamation point (!)** to end a sentence that expresses strong feelings:

- Wow! That story is really long!

Punctuation *(continued)*

Use a **comma** (**,**) after the salutation (greeting) of an informal letter and the closing of a letter:

- Dear Uncle Chris **,**
- Yours truly **,**

Use a **comma** (**,**) to separate:

a city and state, or a city and country	El Paso **,** Texas London **,** England **Note:** Also use a comma *after* the state or country in a sentence. Coloma **,** California **,** is where gold was discovered in 1849.
the date from the year	October 12 **,** 2004 **Note:** In a sentence, use a comma before and after the year. October 24 **,** 1929 **,** was the start of the Great Depression.

two adjectives that tell about the same noun	Nico is a witty **,** smart boy.
	
	Hint: Use these two "tests" to see if you need the comma:
	
	1. Switch the order of the adjectives. If the sentence has the same meaning and still makes sense, you must use a comma.
	
	    Nico is a smart, witty boy. (This is the same as *Nico is a witty, smart boy.*)
	    Nico has dark brown hair. (It doesn't make sense to say *Nico has brown dark hair,* so no comma is needed.)
	
	2. Put the word "and" between the two adjectives. If the sentence still makes sense, you must use a comma.
	
	    Nico is a witty, smart boy. (This is the same as *Nico is a witty and smart boy.*)
	    Nico has dark brown hair. (It doesn't make sense to say *Nico has dark and brown hair.*)

items in a list or series (with three or more items)	Sarah won't eat beets **,** spinach **,** or shrimp.
the name of the person that someone is addressing and the information that he or she is giving	Sam **,** I think that you should spend less money. I think that you should spend less money **,** Sam. I think **,** Sam **,** that you should spend less money.

Daily Paragraph Editing • EMC 2837 • © Evan-Moor Corp.

Punctuation *(continued)*

Use a **comma** (**,**) to signify a pause:

between a quotation and the rest of the sentence	Mrs. Flores said, "It's time to break the piñata now!" "I know," answered Maya.
after an interjection at the beginning of a sentence	Boy, that's a lot of candy! Oh well, I misjudged.
after a short introductory word or phrase that comes before the main idea of a sentence	Clearly, no one wants dessert. After all that candy, nobody was hungry for cake.
before and after a word or phrase that interrupts the main idea of a sentence	The cake, however, was already on the picnic table.
before and after a phrase that renames or gives more information about the noun that precedes it	Mrs. Lutz, our neighbor, gave Mom the recipe. The cake, which had thick chocolate frosting, melted in the hot sun.
before the conjunction (*and, but, for, nor, or, so, yet*) in a compound sentence	The frosting was melted, but the cake was great. **Note:** A complete sentence includes a <u>subject</u> and a <u>verb</u>, and it expresses a complete thought. A compound sentence joins two simple sentences with a conjunction; each of the two parts of a compound sentence has its own <u>subject</u> and <u>verb</u>. Maya <u>likes</u> the beach, but <u>she</u> <u>prefers</u> the mountains. **But:** Maya <u>likes</u> the beach but prefers the mountains.

Use a **semicolon** (**;**) to join two simple sentences that are closely related:

- The party ended at 4:00; the guests left by 4:15.

- The party was great fun; however, the cleanup was exhausting.

Use a **colon** (**:**) as follows:

to introduce a list of items	The café has a few specialties: soup, salad, and dessert.
to introduce a sentence, a question, or a quotation	The principal asked an important question: Who will host the Book Fair while the librarian is on vacation?
to show time	The bell rings at 8:20, 12:35, and 3:35 on school days.

Punctuation *(continued)*

Use **quotation marks** (" "):

before and after dialogue (words spoken by someone)	"This was the best birthday party ever!" Maya said. **Note:** A period at the end of a sentence with dialogue always goes inside the quotation marks. A question mark or an exclamation point that follows what the speaker says also goes inside quotation marks. Maya's sister agreed, "Everyone had fun." "May I have a piñata at my birthday party?" Martin asked. Mr. Flores replied, "You bet!" **Be careful!** When the words that tell who is speaking come *before* the quotation, put the comma outside the quotation marks. When the words that tell who is speaking come *after* the quotation, put the comma inside the quotation marks. **Before:** Mrs. Flores asked, "Do you want chocolate cake?" **After:** "I sure do," said Martin.
around a word or phrase being discussed	The word "piñata" is written with a special letter.
around an expression or a word used in an unusual or ironic way	She was "down to the wire" turning in her history essay. Ben thinks the carousel is a "children's" ride.
around the definition of a word	The Latin word <u>geologia</u> means "the study of the earth."

Use an **apostrophe** (') to show possession.

When there is just one owner, add an apostrophe first and then add **s**.	cat + 's ⟶ cat's	The cat's dish was empty.
When there is more than one owner, just add an apostrophe after the plural **s** (unless the plural word is irregular, as with the words *children* and *people*).	cats + ' ⟶ cats' **But:**	All of the cats' cages at the shelter were large. The children's cat was in the last cage. Other people's pets were making lots of noise.

Use an **apostrophe** (') when you put two words together to make a contraction:

- I + am ⟶ I'm
- do + not ⟶ don't

Daily Paragraph Editing • EMC 2837 • © Evan-Moor Corp.

Punctuation *(continued)*

Use a **hyphen** (**-**):

between numbers in a fraction	One-half of the candies have walnuts, and one-quarter have almonds.
to join two words that form an adjective that usually comes before a noun	Beth eats low-fat foods and drinks sugar-free beverages.

Use **parentheses** (( )):

to set off a word or words that interrupt, explain, or qualify a main idea in a sentence but that are not essential to the sentence	Many U.S. households (about 40 percent) have dogs as pets. **Note:** If the interruption comes at the end of a sentence, place the end punctuation after the closing parenthesis. If it comes after a phrase that ends with a comma, place the comma after the closing parenthesis. Dogs are popular pets (although cats are also popular). I didn't like the main course (which was grilled tofu), but I ate it anyway.
to set off a nonessential sentence in a paragraph	Dogs are popular pets. (Cats are also popular.) **Note:** The end punctuation goes inside the parentheses.

Use **brackets** (**[ ]**) to set off a word or words that are enclosed by parentheses:

- Jill loved the band (especially the lead singer, Jeff [always dressed in wild, eccentric outfits], who also played guitar) that she saw Saturday night.

Note: Use punctuation with brackets in the same way you would use punctuation with parentheses.

Use **ellipses** (**. . .**) for a pause or break:

- I couldn't understand the math problem . . . until my friend Angie helped me.

Language Usage

A **plural noun** names more than one person, place, or thing.

If the noun ends in *y*, change the *y* to *i* and add *es*.	fly ⟶ fli + **es** ⟶ fli**es** story ⟶ stori + **es** ⟶ stori**es**	
Some plural nouns are irregular.	child ⟶ children man ⟶ men woman ⟶ women	person ⟶ people tooth ⟶ teeth goose ⟶ geese

An **adverb** describes action.

Some adjectives can be changed to adverbs with **ly**.	awkward ⟶ awkward + **ly** ⟶ awkwardly quick ⟶ quick + **ly** ⟶ quickly
Some common adverbs do not end in **ly**.	He ran **fast**. We worked **harder** than ever before. The girls sang **high** but the boys sang **low**. The book was **well** worth reading.

Sentence Structure

A **modifier** is a word, phrase, or clause that describes another word, phrase, or clause. A modifier that is separated from the word or words that it modifies is called a **misplaced modifier**.

Wrongly placed adverbs such as *only*, *just*, and *almost* can change the meaning of a sentence. **Hint:** Identify the modifier. Then ask yourself which word in the sentence you want to modify.	I have only a dozen eggs. (In this example, *only* modifies a *dozen*.) I only have a dozen eggs. (In this example, *only* modifies *have*.) Only I have a dozen eggs. (In this example, *only* modifies *I*.)
Wrongly placed phrases can be confusing (and even funny).	The children left to play video games **on their bikes**. **Change to:** The children on their bikes left to play video games.

A **dangling modifier** is a phrase or clause that does not logically agree with the word or words that it seems to modify. Note how each sentence has been edited to fix the dangling modifier.

Stashed away in a drawer, he forgot his textbook. (It was the textbook, not the boy, that was in a drawer!)	⟶	He forgot his textbook, which was stashed away in a drawer.
To get the job, an application needs to be filled out. (It's a person, not the application, that wants the job!)	⟶	To get the job, you need to fill out an application.

Daily Paragraph Editing • EMC 2837 • © Evan-Moor Corp.